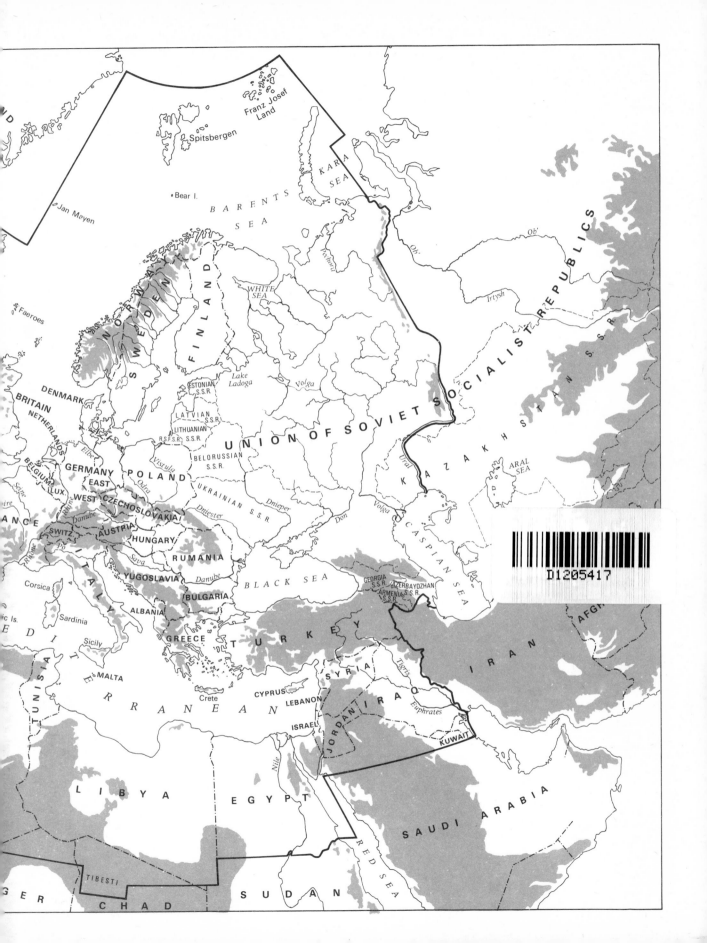

Wildfowl of
Britain and Europe

Wildfowl of Britain and Europe

Malcolm Ogilvie

Paintings by
N. W. Cusa and
Peter Scott

Oxford New York
OXFORD UNIVERSITY PRESS
1982

Oxford University Press, Walton Street, Oxford OX2 6DP

London Glasgow New York Toronto
Delhi Bombay Calcutta Madras Karachi
Kuala Lumpur Singapore Hong Kong Tokyo
Nairobi Dar es Salaam Cape Town
Melbourne Auckland
and associates in
Beirut Berlin Ibadan Mexico City Nicosia

Published in the United States
by Oxford University Press, New York

British Library Cataloguing in Publication Data
Ogilvie, Malcolm
Wildfowl of Britain and Europe.
1. Water-birds — Europe
I. Title
598.4'1   QL696.A5
ISBN 0-19-217723-0

Library of Congress Cataloging in Publication Data
Ogilvie, Malcolm Alexander.
  Wildfowl of Britain and Europe.

  Includes index.
  1. Waterfowl — Great Britain — Identification.
2. Waterfowl — Europe — Identification. 3. Birds —
Identification. 4. Birds — Great Britain — Identification.
5. Birds — Europe — Identification. I. Title.
QL696.A520363 1982   *598.4'1094   82–12402*
ISBN 0–19–217723–0

Set by Oxford Publishing Services
Printed in Hong Kong

Foreword

by Stanley Cramp

The ducks, geese, and swans, often popularly known as wildfowl, form a natural grouping, a single Family Anatidae in the Order Anseriformes. There are some 140 species in the world, of which 54 are found in Europe. They have long had a strong appeal to human beings, for they are colourful and evocative of wild places—and many of them also provide excellent eating, whether shot as one of the favourite quarries of the hunter, kept semidomesticated as the Mute Swans in Britain in the Middle Ages, or fully domesticated as our farmyard geese and ducks. They have been intensively studied by ornithologists, especially in recent years, and much is known of their behaviour, numbers, movements, and food. The aim of this work is to illustrate their variety and beauty, and to summarize the main aspects of their biology, which, despite their close relationship, exhibits an often astonishing diversity. The plates, by N. W. Cusa and Sir Peter Scott, are taken from the first volume of the *Handbook of the Birds of Europe, North Africa, and the Middle East: The Birds of the Western Palearctic* (1977), a seven-volume work now being published by the Oxford University Press. The text is by Malcolm Ogilvie, a research worker at the Wildfowl Trust, Slimbridge, and the author of several books on wildfowl. He is also one of the Editors of *The Birds of the Western Palearctic*, on which his text is largely based and which readers who desire fuller information on any aspect should consult.

Ducks, geese, and swans live in or near water, usually fresh or brackish but sometimes marine. They nest in or near wetland areas normally on the ground but also in burrows or holes in trees. These wetland areas are found in Europe from the northern tundras and forests, through the temperate latitudes to the shores of the Mediterranean. After breeding, many wildfowl move to more southern wetland areas. Virtually all the more northern species move south to winter on unfrozen waters, though most remain then in Europe; many nesting in more temperate latitudes need to travel smaller distances, though some fly as far as Africa, while the most southern species tend to be largely sedentary, except when droughts force them to make local movements. But whatever the species, without wetlands for nesting, on passage or in winter, they cannot survive.

Yet these essential wetlands face a diversity of threats throughout Europe. The northern tundras and forests, where most swans and geese and many ducks nest, cover a vast area still little disturbed, and though full breeding censuses are impossible, counts in the wintering areas, organized by the International Waterfowl Research Bureau and carried out by thousands of amateur birdwatchers, suggest that numbers of most northern wildfowl are being maintained; some, like the Brent Goose, have increased markedly in recent years. So the wetland habitats there appear not to be at risk yet, but farther south in the temperate belt stretching across western and central Europe the situation is very different. Drainage of wetlands there has been carried out for centuries and has been steadily intensified in recent years; now, most of the remaining wetland areas are small and scattered, so that safe nesting sites are much more limited, while the far greater numbers and variety of species which use them on migration and in winter face a possibly catastrophic decline in the feeding and resting places essential for their survival. In southern Europe, wetlands have always been less numerous and more scattered, but these, too, are now being drained on an alarming scale. Moreover, many key estuaries, especially in north-west Europe, are also threatened by industrial developments.

Wildfowl have been hunted throughout human history. While a few species outside Europe (e.g. the Labrador Duck and Pink-headed Duck) may have been brought to extinction by excessive hunting in the past, most conservationists and all responsible hunters would now agree that such hunting is a legitimate sport only if it is so regulated that the populations of the quarry species are not adversely affected. This implies that hunting is controlled by various means—e.g. a complete ban on some species, close seasons for others (during breeding and often also when migrating), the prohibition of some weapons, licences, restrictions on sale, and sometimes bag limits. There are considerable variations in national and local regulations in Europe, but generally speaking, most geese and ducks (but few swans) are hunted in the majority of countries. For all these quarry species, it is essential that population trends are carefully monitored and that much fuller information on hunting kills and sales is obtained. Hunting may have other undesirable effects on populations in addition to direct killing, e.g. crippling of birds so that they die later of starvation, poisoning by lead shot, and disturbance which may prevent them having sufficient food or rest if adequate refuges are not provided. For most of the commoner quarry species, hunting at present levels in Europe does not seem to be a serious danger; for others, especially those already declining because of habitat change or vulnerability to oil pollution (as in most sea-ducks), some reduction in hunting pressures needs consideration. The fruitful collaboration between hunters and conservationists on such problems, which has developed markedly in recent years in Britain and other countries, must be strengthened and extended.

Habitat change, however, probably remains the most serious danger to many wildfowl. In recent years a number of international conventions (the Ramsar Convention on wetlands, the Bonn Convention on migrating animals, the EEC Directive on the conservation of wild birds) have taken the first steps towards the adequate conservation of wetlands. They need to be implemented vigorously and more widely adopted if the numbers and variety of European wildfowl are to be maintained in an increasingly man-dominated world.

Contents

An introduction to the wildfowl

Introduction and classification

The family of birds known as the wildfowl are popularly divided into the swans, the geese, and the ducks. This division suggests that these three groups are perhaps equal in size within the family. However, this is very far from being so. The different kinds of ducks easily outnumber the total of swans and geese combined. Within the area covered by this book, Europe, with North Africa and the Middle East (see map—endpapers), there are three species of swans, ten of geese, and 41 of ducks, a total of 54. It might also be thought that the swans, geese, and ducks bear roughly equal relationships towards each other. This, too, does not reflect the true situation. The swans and geese are much more closely related than are many of the different kinds of ducks. For a better understanding of the wildfowl it is necessary to look briefly at the hierarchy of subdivisions into which they are classified.

The wildfowl are placed in a separate family with the scientific name Anatidae. This is one of two families in the higher classification, the Order Anseriformes. The other family is a very small one containing just three species of birds called Screamers, confined to the grasslands of South America. The Anatidae can be distinguished from other birds in many ways. They are all waterbirds, though several of them also feed on land, with relatively short legs, compared to, say, the waders or herons, and all have webbing between their toes. Outwardly at least they show enormous variation in size, shape, and plumage colouring. For example, within our area the largest wildfowl, the Mute Swan, can weigh up to 22.5 kg, while the smallest, the Bufflehead and the Teal, generally weigh between 250 and 400 g. The swans have greatly elongated necks, the stifftails very short

ones. Plumage colour varies from all-white swans, or virtually all-black Brent Geese, to most remarkably patterned birds like the Mandarin or Harlequin. Yet all these birds have enough similarities, especially perhaps in their anatomy, to justify grouping them into the one family.

Without going into anatomical detail, a few of the major areas which bear out this grouping of all the wildfowl into one family can be mentioned; others will become apparent as the family and its various subdivisions are described. The bill is entirely characteristic of wildfowl, being unlike that of any other birds. It is highly variable in size and shape, depending on adaptations to different foods by the different species, but the essential components are the same throughout. The bill is covered with a thin layer of skin, and possesses a horny plate at the tip, called the 'nail', after its likeness to a finger-nail. At the edges of the mandibles are rows of lamellae, tooth-like projections used for grasping food. The tongue, too, is covered with small protrusions, and bordered with horny spines, for the same purpose. Internally there are certain features of the skeleton and musculature which are shared by all the wildfowl. The feathering on the body is arranged in defined tracts. It is thick and waterproof, and additionally has a thick layer of down lying underneath the external layer of feathers, to provide further insulation against the cold water. It is also used by most species as a lining for their nests, being plucked by the female from her breast. There are a constant eleven primary feathers, though the number of secondaries and tail feathers, fixed in many kinds of birds, is variable.

The family Anatidae is generally divided into three subfamilies, of which two, the Anserinae, containing the swans and the geese, and the Anatinae, containing all the ducks, are represented in our area. The Anserinae have rather long necks, and the legs are placed near the middle of the body, so that the birds stand fairly upright. The legs, seen close to, have a fine network of scales on the front. There is little or no difference between males and females of any of the species in this subfamily. The Anatinae tend to be shorter in the neck and legs, and to have the latter positioned nearer the tail. The front of the legs have parallel rows of scales not a network pattern. In most, though not all, species, the males have a colourful plumage, while the females are rather dull and well camouflaged.

Below the subfamily comes the tribe. There are 12 tribes of wildfowl (though some experts have reduced this to ten or even nine) split between the three subfamilies. Four of them do not have any representation in the area covered by this book. It is at this level that the various species begin to fit together into recognizable groups, and a brief review of the tribes and their characteristics will conclude this section on classification.

Tribe Anserini: swans and true geese

The largest wildfowl are grouped in this tribe, the swans and what are known as the 'true' geese, to distinguish them from other wildfowl whose popular names include the word 'goose' but which are not in fact closely related. The birds all have powerful bills, well adapted for grazing on plants, on land and in the water. Their plumage is the same in both male and female, and lacks any iridescent colouring, or any contrasting pattern on the wing, both of which are possessed by species in other tribes. Their downy young lack any patterning, being at most a little darker above, paler below.

There are three species of swans in Europe, the Mute, Whooper, and Bewick's, and ten geese, Bean, Pink-footed, White-fronted, Lesser White-fronted, Greylag, Snow, Canada, Barnacle, Brent, and Red-breasted.

Tribe Tadornini: shelducks and sheldgeese

Despite the occurrence of the word 'geese' in the name for some species in this tribe, they are, in fact, more closely related to the ducks than to the true geese of the tribe Anserini. They are certainly quite goose-like in shape and stance. The species

occurring in our area, however, have more duck-like bills, flattened on the top. The males and females can be identical in plumage, or show some differences. Nearly all of them have bold white patches on the upper and under sides of their wings, and an iridescent green speculum. The downy young are strongly patterned in black and white.

In our area this tribe is represented by the Egyptian Goose, the Shelduck, and the Ruddy Shelduck.

Tribe Cairini: perching ducks

There is immense variation in this family across the world, with some very large goose-like species, and other quite tiny ducks. They share the ability, and frequent habit, of perching on branches and other prominences. Many of them have much iridescent plumage on their body, sometimes in both sexes, as the plumage of the male and female can be the same. Many species nest in cavities in rocks or holes in trees, and their downy young are noted for their ability to climb, having sharp claws and relatively long, stiff tails. This enables them to climb out of holes and reach the ground within a day or two of hatching. The downy young patterns are generally rather like those of the dabbling ducks, indicating a fairly close relationship.

There is just one perching duck in our area, the introduced Mandarin Duck from China.

Tribe Anatini: dabbling ducks

This group includes ducks with fairly broad flattened bills adapted to feeding on the water surface, or sometimes on land. Their legs are set quite near the middle of the body giving them a horizontal stance. Although most species can dive, none does so very efficiently or for long. Unlike those ducks which are adapted for diving and swimming underwater, the hind toe of dabbling ducks is small and not lobed. They can rise without difficulty from the water, walk readily on land, and can perch, though few do so regularly. The males are brightly coloured for most of the year, adopting a dull 'eclipse' plumage for the period of the annual wing moult. The females are a dull well-camouflaged brown throughout the year. Virtually all the species have a brightly coloured iridescent speculum on the wing. The downy young are conspicuously patterned in brown and yellow, usually with a darker cap to the head and a dark stripe through the eye.

The dabbling ducks of the region number 13, namely Wigeon, American Wigeon, Falcated Teal, Gadwall, Teal, Cape Teal, Mallard, Black Duck, Pintail, Garganey, Blue-winged Teal, Shoveler, and Marbled Teal.

Tribe Aythini: pochards

These birds are often known as diving ducks, but there are others which qualify for that description. The point of difference, though, is that the pochards are nearly all freshwater diving ducks. They have short, heavy bodies, and typically take off from the water only after a pattering run over the surface. The legs are set well back on the body, ideally adapted for diving and swimming under water, but making for rather clumsy movements on land. The webbed feet have rather broad toes, and the hind toe is quite large and lobed. Underwater propulsion is by feet alone. Plumage colouring is generally rather dull, including the males, and iridescent plumage is rare. There is no iridescent speculum, for example. Males and females differ. The downy young resemble the young of Anatini, but the eyestripe is either faint or lacking altogether.

Six species of these freshwater diving ducks occur in the area, Red-crested Pochard, Pochard, Ring-necked Duck, Ferruginous Duck, Tufted Duck, and Scaup.

Tribe Somaterini: eiders

The eiders are marine diving ducks with broad heavy bodies, though longer than the pochards', and with relatively large heads. The powerful legs are set well back, though eiders can walk on land if with a rolling gait and the body held rather upright. Underwater, the wings are used more than the legs in swimming, being opened a short distance and then closed with short jerking movements. Male eiders are very boldly patterned in black and white, together with some areas of soft pastel tones. The females are all a well-camouflaged brown. The males become rather female-like during their annual wing moult. The downy young are distinctively marked, being brown above with a dark line through the eye, and paler below.

The four species to occur in Europe are the Eider, King Eider, Spectacled Eider, and Steller's Eider.

Tribe Mergini: scoters, sawbills, and other sea-ducks

These are all marine diving ducks, quite closely related to the eiders and sharing some of their characteristics. Some are awkward on land, others more able. Some species use their wings for moving underwater, others are more like the Aythini and use only their legs and feet. With the exception of the wholly black Common Scoter, all the males are black and white, though the proportions of each vary enormously. Most species have some white on the wing, but only the Harlequin has a metallic speculum. The females are generally brown, brown and white, or grey and white. The majority of the downy young have a dark cap and pale cheek, and are paler below than above.

The European Mergini number 12, and are Harlequin, Long-tailed Duck, Common Scoter, Surf Scoter, Velvet Scoter, Bufflehead, Barrow's Goldeneye, Goldeneye, Hooded Merganser, Smew, Red-breasted Merganser, and Goosander.

Tribe Oxyurini: stiff-tailed ducks

The final tribe of the wildfowl comprises the stiff-tailed ducks. They are all rather small or medium-sized ducks with short bodies and short thick necks. Their name comes from the remarkable long, narrow tail of stiffened feathers which acts as a rudder underwater. They are accomplished divers with their large feet set so far back on their bodies that walking on land becomes very difficult, indeed little more than a shuffle. Taking off from the water is very laboured. Males and females differ, but brightly coloured plumage and iridescence are lacking. The downy young typically show a head pattern of dark brown, and an eyestripe that is similar to that of the adult female.

The White-headed Duck and the Ruddy Duck are the two stifftails occurring in our area.

Evolution and hybridization

Throughout the natural world evolution is continually in progress, and the wildfowl are affected by this in a number of ways. Whilst the formation of a new species or even subspecies occurs far too slowly for us to be aware of it, wildfowl are constantly adapting to new circumstances in their environment, new habitats, and especially new foods, which are tiny steps on the path of evolution.

For example, the Pink-footed Goose in Britain has discovered a completely new food in the last hundred years, which now forms an important part of its diet. The natural food of these geese includes grass and other short vegetation which they graze, grasping the leaves with the edges of their bills, where they are held between the lamellae on each mandible. In the latter part of the last century, fields of potatoes in Lancashire were left unharvested following severe attacks of potato blight. The Pinkfeet feeding on the grasslands and on the stubbles of harvested corn fields in that area discovered that the potatoes were a good food. It is not known quite how this came about, but perhaps they were attracted to a potato field by the sight of other birds, such as Mallard, already feeding there.

The potato-eating habit remained among the Pinkfeet and gradually spread to other parts of the country, until now it occurs wherever the distribution of the geese and of potato-growing overlap. The birds wait until the crop has been harvested and then move on to the fields, and glean the small tubers and broken pieces left on the ground. Fragments of potato can be picked up and swallowed whole, but larger pieces and whole tubers have to be dealt with differently. The nail of the bill is used to scoop out thin slivers, helped by the tongue and the lamellae. This adoption of a new food, and a method of dealing with it, may not seem very important in itself, but over the years it must have made some difference to the population of Pinkfeet, by providing an additional supply of food, and therefore enabling any given area to support more geese. Those birds which learnt to exploit the potatoes were potentially more able to survive than those which did not. In this way a tiny evolutionary change took place, which might not be measurable by itself, but taken with other adaptations could gradually have an important effect on the success of that particular species. On the whole those birds which show themselves capable of readily adapting to changing circumstances are more likely to succeed than those which cannot.

The Pink-footed Goose can be used to demonstrate how some species of wildfowl have evolved into different subspecies or races, and how it is possible to suggest which other species may be embarking on the same road. The Pinkfoot is, clearly, from its external and internal features, very closely related to the Bean Goose. The latter has evolved into five identifiable subspecies, which differ in overall size, and particularly in the size and shape of the bill. There are also racial differences in the amount of orange present on the otherwise black bill. Each race has its own breeding area within the overall range across northern Eurasia, though with some overlap and indeed intergrading where they meet. The Pink-footed Goose's range lies at the western end of the Bean Goose's and many taxonomists have considered it merely another race of the Bean Goose.

It can be assumed that an original Bean Goose stock gradually populated the entire present range, presumably as the conditions permitted at the end of the last ice age. Because the breeding range is so great, subpopulations began to form within it, each having its own traditional breeding range, from which they departed along different migration routes, and so found themselves in often widely separated winter quarters. Geese are highly traditional birds and over succeeding generations this pattern would have been reinforced. Very gradually environmental factors and adaptations led to small but distinct differences beginning to appear between birds of the different populations, until today we can clearly identify five subspecies of the Bean Goose. The Pinkfoot, although clearly coming from the same original Bean Goose stock, has managed to evolve further than the other races, until it is recognized by most authorities as a full species.

There are other examples, particularly among the geese, of subspecies developing from a common stock. For example, the White-fronted Geese have evolved four or five subspecies, two of which, the European and Greenland Whitefronts, occur in the West Palearctic, the others in North America. The much smaller Lesser Whitefront is a different species, but clearly came from a common ancestor with the Whitefront.

Just as intriguing, perhaps, is to look at those species which have not yet evolved any distinct differences, yet are living in circumstances which could well lead to such a development. The Barnacle Goose, for example, occurs in three completely discrete populations, breeding in East Greenland, Spitsbergen, and north-west arctic USSR. They winter in three separate areas, the western coasts of Scotland and Ireland, the Solway Firth between England and Scotland, and in the Netherlands, respectively. None of these areas is far apart, less than 180 km separates the Solway Firth from the Inner Hebrides, but mixing of the stocks is virtually unknown, as large-scale marking has shown. Outwardly all the Barnacle Geese from the three populations are identical. The only difference that has been detected is in the average weights, though there is considerable overlap. There are no discernible differences in measurements. If there is a weight difference, it may well be the first minute indication that evolution is taking its course. The separation of the three populations may only be of the order of hundreds or a thousand or two years. If they remain separate for a rather longer period then obvious changes may occur, leading eventually to three races of Barnacle Goose as distinct as are the Bean Goose and Whitefront races today.

A textbook answer to the question 'What is a species?' might be that a species does not interbreed with any other kind of organism. Interbreeding, or hybridization, is however, quite common among some birds, and probably nowhere more so than among the wildfowl. Much of it arises when birds of many different kinds are kept in captivity, in circumstances where there may not be the freedom of movement and choice of mate that would exist in the wild. Birds thrown into close contact with others in an artificial way may make unusual pairings. However, hybrid pairs also form in the wild, generally though between birds that are closely related, whereas in captivity some of the pairings may be between birds from widely separated tribes within the family of wildfowl. The occurrence of these hybrids might seem to throw doubt on the concept of species separation. It is probably better to regard them as evidence that all the wildfowl are reasonably closely related within their family. Hybrids between wildfowl and birds of other families are unknown.

Hybrids could easily be ignored by the average birdwatcher if it were not for the fact that some of them, and this seems particularly so with wildfowl hybrids, cause considerable identification problems by being confused with genuine species. The chief difficulty arises with hybrids from within the tribe Aythini, the Pochards. This group seems particularly prone to hybridizations, perhaps because the males are not highly differentiated in their plumage, while their courtship displays directed at the females are very similar. Birdwatchers do like to know what they are looking at and become understandably frustrated when confronted with a diving duck which may look very like some interesting rare species, perhaps a vagrant from North America, and yet not be quite right in every particular.

It is a curious fact, and one that has caused birdwatchers a lot of trouble, that some male hybrids resulting from the pairing of a male Tufted Duck and a female Pochard, look extremely like a Lesser Scaup, a small North American diving duck which has never been reliably reported in Europe. The result of a pairing between a female Tufted Duck and a male Pochard, on the other hand, looks quite different, much more like a Tufted Duck.

Other diving ducks which can be closely resembled by some hybrids are Ferruginous Duck and Baer's Pochard. The former is a vagrant to Britain from east and south Europe, the latter is confined to the Far East.

A further problem is caused by hybrids between one of the vagrant species and a commoner one. Thus hybrids have been reported between the Ring-necked Duck, another North American diving duck which occasionally does wander to Europe, and Tufted Ducks. It is quite possible that these were bred in captivity. However, it could be that a genuine wild Ring-necked Duck crossed the Atlantic and then stayed in Europe, pairing and breeding with the nearest relative it could find, in the absence of any others of its own kind. This is actually known to have happened with the North American Black Duck, a female of which arrived on the Scilly Isles one year and stayed on, to breed in subsequent years with a male Mallard. Unfortunately the hybrids could be confused with Black Ducks, and this must cast doubt on future records of this species, certainly from south-west England and perhaps from further afield.

Hybrids among other groups of wildfowl, for example the geese, occur quite frequently in captivity, though rather rarely in the wild. Apparent hybrids between European Whitefront and

Lesser Whitefront have been seen from time to time in the wild, while crosses between feral or semiferal Canada Geese and Greylags occur in a number of places where the two breed side by side. Unlike the diving ducks, goose hybrids are immediately recognizable for what they are, as well as generally being rather unattractive in appearance!

Occasional male King Eiders are sometimes seen in the large Eider colonies of Iceland. Pairs are sometimes formed between these and female Eiders and the resulting hybrids then turn up a couple of years later, though usually only the males are recognizable. Fortunately, perhaps, wildfowl hybrids are not particularly fertile, and unless someone with captive birds deliberately tries to breed from them, the chances of succeeding generations of hybrids occurring is not very great. Any birdwatcher, though, confronted with a duck or goose he is not quite sure of, and perhaps showing most though not quite all of the characters of a particular species, should bear in mind the possibility that he is looking at a hybrid.

Habitat

A bird's habitat must provide it with sufficient food, safety from its enemies, perhaps particularly at night, and suitable nesting sites. That wildfowl obtain all three by their use of water is probably something which hardly needs saying. Yet, of course, water, and particularly the wetland habitat associated with it, exists in enormous variety. It is a measure of the success of wildfowl as a group that they have evolved to take advantage of nearly every different type of wetland, both fresh and salt. Then again, some wildfowl are far more aquatic than others, so that their use of the land varies too. Within our area, wildfowl have adapted to using the full range of habitat zones available to them, from the high arctic tundra and coasts in the north to the saline lakes on the desert fringes in the south.

Freshwater habitat can first be classified as eutrophic or oligotrophic. The former is fertile, with the water tending to be alkaline and containing plenty of calcium, nitrogen, and phosphorous, available to the plankton and water plants on which other life depends. Oligotrophic waters, on the other hand, are usually acid, and contain very few nutrients. Consequently growth of animal or plant life is severely restricted. There are some other water types, but not of such essential importance as this major division.

Not surprisingly most wildfowl prefer eutrophic waters, where there is ample food, both animal and plant. There is usually also an abundant growth of emergent vegetation providing the birds with suitable nest sites. Such waters tend to be in the lowlands, away from the largely acid rocks which make up most of the uplands of northern Europe. Lowland eutrophic waters would once have been comprised of natural lakes, river floods, and fenland. All of these have been greatly reduced in number and extent through drainage and reclamation, and it is perhaps fortunate that man's drinking water reservoirs and flooded gravel workings have to some extent replaced them. The main drawback to lowland waters is that the lowlands are also the most densely populated areas of Europe, so the birds have of necessity to adapt to living reasonably close to man, or man has actively to protect them. Both things occur, and even concrete-lined urban reservoirs attract and hold wildfowl.

The majority of the dabbling ducks breed around fresh water and spend the rest of the year on it too. The same is true for the diving ducks, each having its own preferred niche of area and depth of water for feeding, of food, and of nest-site, enabling several species to live in the same wetland. Geese and swans also use lowland eutrophic waters for roosting at night and for some feeding, though also moving out to surrounding farmland and marshes for food.

Oligotrophic lakes hold rather few wildfowl, unless at night-time for roosting, and then only if there are suitable feeding grounds within a reasonable distance. Many such lakes are very large and deep, contain little food, and can produce a considerable wave action in windy weather, all of which act against their use by wildfowl. Only where the pools are small, can a few birds settle, perhaps breeding pairs of Lesser Whitefront, Bean Goose, Wigeon, or Teal, one or two in the vicinity of each pool. Over large areas of such habitat, wet moorland or in the forested areas of northern Europe, where small pools and bogs abound among the trees, a fair population of birds may exist, though everywhere at a very low density.

Rivers and streams may be eutrophic or oligotrophic in nature, depending on the underlying rocks and soil through which they are flowing. Rather few wildfowl are adapted to living in fast running water, mainly the fish-eaters such as Goosander and Red-breasted Merganser, or specialist feeders like the Harlequin, as vegetable food is not generally available in quantity. Where nest holes are available then Smew and Goldeneye may also be found. In the lower reaches of rivers, where they become very similar in character to linear lakes, similar kinds of birds will be living, though in any inhabited land there is considerable interference with most rivers, as they are kept within their banks, dredged and used by boats, and quite probably polluted.

On the arctic tundra, small pools and shallow lakes are plentiful, the water unable to drain away because of the underlying permafrost. Where there is any soil fertility the resulting vegetation and animal life will provide food for Bewick's Swans, Pink-footed, Barnacle, and Brent Geese as well as, in the low arctic at least, Wigeon, Teal, Pintail, Tufted Duck, and Scaup. Nesting places may be in the vegetation, or where this is too short, on rocky outcrops, small islets, or even some distance away on inland cliff ledges, a perhaps unlikely site occupied by Barnacle Geese as a defence against arctic foxes.

Sheltered estuaries and low-lying coastal mudflats are the home for several species of wildfowl, some of which also occur on inland fresh waters. The Shelduck is wholly restricted to such habitat throughout the year. Nests are placed in any suitable hole, natural or artificial, and can be some distance inland, but the young are always brought to the mudflats to be reared. All of the animal food is found in the mud, which must be exposed by the tide or covered only with very shallow water. The same is true for the food of the Brent Goose, which lives in just the same habitat, grazing on marine grasses and algae growing on the mud and sand. Teal, Mallard, Pintail, and Wigeon, are all found on estuaries, though many may move inland, or at least on to the saltings for food. Wide open spaces provide excellent sanctuary. However, in the shooting season, disturbance may drive many birds inland for shorter or longer periods. It is this that seems to have been the reason for many goose flocks to have changed their night-time roosting places from estuaries to inland waters.

The more open sea coast can be occupied only by birds which can obtain their food underwater. Some, like the eiders, the Scaup, and the scoters, eat shellfish and crustaceans from the bottom of the sea, diving to a few metres depth to reach them. Others, like the sawbills, are fish-eaters, so that the depth of water is not the same problem, provided the upper layers of the sea contain sufficient fish. The eiders are more or less restricted to the coasts for breeding as well as for the remainder of the year, but the scoters, and the Long-tailed Duck, may breed on the coast or far inland, only returning to the sea when their young have fledged. On the whole the distribution of the food and the roughness of the water prevent wildfowl from living very many kilometres from the coast. Only where there are extensive areas of shallow, more or less protected or enclosed seas, will this occur, as for example in the area between Denmark and Sweden, and further into the Baltic, or on a smaller scale in the Moray Firth in north-east Scotland.

Distribution, numbers, and mortality

Brief notes on the distribution and numbers of each wildfowl species in the area covered by this book can be found in the text facing each relevant plate. As a background to those it is possible to make some more general statements on the subject and to look at the major causes of death in wildfowl and how these affect the overall pattern of numbers and population trends.

The present day distribution of wildfowl is very greatly influenced by man and his activities. The particular requirements for breeding wildfowl, especially those needing fresh water, may once have been found throughout the temperate zone but as this became the region most heavily populated by humans so the landscape changed and the area of fresh water decreased. Simultaneously hunting and disturbance pressures reduced the attractiveness of the area at other times of the year. We cannot know in detail how wildfowl populations were affected by such changes but the picture now is for the great majority of wildfowl in the West Palearctic to breed in the boreal and arctic zones to the north. As discussed in the Habitat section, the boreal zone, while forested, is rich in pools and streams, while the arctic tundra contains extensive areas of marsh. To some extent at least wildfowl must have been shifted out of the temperate zone northwards into these sparsely inhabited and undisturbed regions, where they found suitable habitat.

The drawback of nesting in northern latitudes is that they become untenable in winter. Whereas breeding wildfowl in temperate regions can for the most part remain there throughout the year, those breeding further north must migrate to warmer areas each autumn and stay there until the following spring. The western parts of Europe, and the Mediterranean and Black Seas provide just such a required wintering area for the breeding birds of the northern part of Europe. A few species migrate further to the great areas of wetland in both West and East Africa.

Although man's occupation of the temperate zone gradually prevented the nesting there of large numbers of wildfowl, the situation in winter was not so drastically affected. Certainly destruction of habitat has a permanent effect, but where suitable areas remained, these could still be used by large numbers of birds. The habitat requirements in winter are not quite so restricting as they are in summer, the birds not in quite such danger as they are when tied to a single spot where their nest is placed. Where birds are shot regularly they can mitigate the effects by becoming very wary, flying high, and sticking to open spaces for roosting and feeding. Extreme wariness is not the natural state for wildfowl, but one brought about by persecution. As is so obvious from the tameness of wild ducks in some of our city parks, if the danger is removed altogether, then the birds have no suspicions of humans, especially not if those humans also provide food.

In recent decades, steadily improving protection has helped to save some populations of wildfowl which might otherwise have disappeared altogether through habitat destruction or over-shooting. The majority of populations of wildfowl in Europe are increasing at the present time, though with some notable exceptions. Some of the more successful and widespread ducks have populations numbered in millions. This is true of several of the dabbling ducks, for example Wigeon, Mallard, and Shoveler, and some of the sea-ducks, such as Eider and Longtail, and perhaps the Common Scoter. These birds either have a catholic choice of habitat or very large areas they can use. The more specialised the bird, the less there is and the fewer its numbers. Even the most numerous of the freshwater diving ducks, the Pochard, has probably only one-third the numbers of the Mallard, requiring as it does always some depth of water, and being unable to exploit shallow marshes or tidal areas. At the other end of the scale among the ducks, there are some very small populations of Marbled Teal and White-headed Duck in the western part of the Mediterranean, though separate populations exist further east.

The larger wildfowl, the swans and the geese, have mostly quite small populations, at least compared with the ducks. Being larger they require more space, both for breeding and wintering. The White-fronted Goose is easily the most numerous, with perhaps half a million in the West Palearctic, though split between a number of discrete populations. Indeed most of the geese and swans can be divided into separate populations, as shown by ringing and by regular counts. This is harder to do with the ducks and where divisions do exist there is often considerable overlap and interchange.

Although there is sometimes cause for concern with very small populations of swans or geese, there are several of under 10 000 which seem quite secure, though needing careful monitoring and usually some protection. Thus there are about 10 000 Bewick's Swans in north-west Europe in winter, while the population of Lesser Whitefronts may be as few as 5000, and is causing some concern because it appears to be decreasing. Discrete populations of Light-bellied Brent Geese include one of about 9000 wintering in Ireland, and a separate one of only 3000, which winters in Denmark and north-east England. Of the three populations of Barnacle Geese, one is about 50 000 strong, a second about 30 000, and a third of only 9000. All these populations have been lower than they are now.

In stable populations, recruitment of young birds each year just about balances mortality. If the population is increasing or decreasing then one or other factor is gaining the upper hand. Recruitment can be said to begin when the clutch of eggs is laid. Losses of eggs can be very high, particularly from predators, and bad weather, well over 50 per cent in some cases, and then the young birds remain extremely vulnerable to these pressures and to starvation in their first few weeks of life. Losses vary enormously from year to year and species to species, but the following examples are not untypical.

Mute Swans studied in Britain over many years lost over 40 per cent of their eggs before hatching, mainly to predation, floods, and vandalism. Of the young which did hatch, 50 per cent died before fledging at about four months old. Starvation was the most important mortality factor, particularly in the first two weeks of life.

Over 40 per cent of Mallard nests at one site in Scotland were destroyed by predators or deserted before hatching. In another area, from a mean clutch size of 11, the mean brood size shortly after hatching was about 7, while the number of young reared by each successful female dropped to under 5.

The hatching success of Eiders in Scotland varied in the course of four years, from just over 50 per cent to over 70 per cent. Much more variable was the fledging rate of the young, from less than 1 per cent to over 40 per cent. The primary mortality factor was thought to be the shortage of food for the very young ducklings.

Once the young birds have successfully fledged the chief cause of death in many species of wildfowl is shooting. Natural mortality is greatly subordinate to this in all the traditional quarry species. Properly regulated, of course, there is no reason why shooting cannot be regarded as taking a legitimate harvest from a population, one that can be and is replaced by the breeding stock which remains at the end of the winter. When there is no shooting then there is probably always a higher natural mortality, particularly of young birds through the winter, from starvation and predation. Many young birds that might otherwise die in the course of the winter are shot in the autumn months.

Natural mortality undoubtedly occurs on the arctic breeding grounds of many species, from periods of very severe weather which the birds are unable to escape, and on migration between breeding and wintering grounds. Many flights are made over the sea for quite long distances, and observations and results from ringing show that the birds may get drifted a long way from their intended course, fetching up in areas where the necessary food and water may not exist in sufficient quantity.

Man has added greatly to the hazards faced by wildfowl, especially perhaps those living on the sea, which have to contend with spilt oil. Deaths of sea-ducks in the Baltic have numbered tens of thousands in some years, and spills around the coasts of the North Sea are becoming almost commonplace. A danger for certain inland species comes from overhead wires. Mute Swans in some areas of Britain have been seriously reduced in numbers because they are unable to avoid wires strung across their accustomed flight paths. Indeed the commonest reported cause of death of Mute Swans ringed in Britain is from flying into wires or some similar obstruction.

Another cause of mortality to come to the fore in recent years has been lead poisoning. There are two sources for the lead. Shot pellets from cartridges fall into the mud and water where ducks are shot, and can then be ingested by feeding birds in mistake for hard seeds or grit, which is used in the gizzard for grinding down the food. Small, heavily shot flight ponds can contain surprisingly high concentrations of pellets, only one of which is enough to kill a duck. Discarded lead weights from fishermen form the other source, and here it is the Mute Swan which seems mainly at risk. Even quite small split shot can kill a swan, while the heavier ledger weights are also eaten and are just as lethal.

The average mortality of young Mallard in their first year of life has been calculated to be as high as 76 per cent in heavily shot areas. Once the birds become adult the mortality drops but may still reach 50–60 per cent per annum. A Mallard reaching the age of one year may have a further life expectancy of only an additional year and a half. This may be contrasted with the annual mortality of the Eider in an area where it is not shot, of about 17 per cent for young birds, reducing to between 2 and 8 per cent per annum for adults, giving them a life expectancy of well over 10 years.

The larger birds can be expected to live longer, though if they are shot this may not be so. Thus the annual mortality of White-fronted Geese is about 30 per cent per annum, while for the protected Barnacle Goose it is only about 8 per cent per annum.

Movements

All the wildfowl species occurring in the area undertake movements in the course of a year, though some populations of a few species are more or less sedentary. Many species and populations are completely migratory, moving between widely separated breeding and wintering grounds, while others may have an overlap between breeding and wintering areas, with some birds resident throughout the year and the remainder migratory.

Most of the introduced populations of wildfowl are sedentary, having lost any instinct for migration. This may be because several generations were kept in captivity before breeding in the wild commenced, or because western Europe where most introductions have taken place is reasonably hospitable throughout the year. The Mandarin Duck, Ruddy Duck, and almost all the Canada Geese introduced into Britain are all migratory in their native ranges, but are sedentary now. The exceptions among the Canada Geese perform a special movement called a 'moult migration' which will be dealt with below. The Canada Geese introduced in southern Sweden do migrate, fairly short distances south to the Baltic, presumably induced by the cold and snow of the Swedish winter. The other species introduced into Britain, the Egyptian Goose, is as sedentary here as it is in Africa. The Ruddy Ducks have shown some movements around western Britain, with flocking on certain waters in the winter, but so far none is known to have left the country.

Many wildfowl breeding in western and southern Europe are sedentary, though there may be highly migratory elements of the same species, which come to these same areas for the winter. The Mallard is easily the most numerous and widespread resident wildfowl in Europe, but the cold of winter drives it out of north and east Europe and the USSR, and these extra birds join the residents, of, for example, the Netherlands, Britain, France, Iberia, Italy, and the Balkans for the winter. Other birds with resident populations include the Greylag, Wigeon, Teal, Pintail, Gadwall, Pochard, Tufted Duck, and Goldeneye. All of these breed in rather small numbers in western Europe, and most of the birds are sedentary or nearly so. All additionally have far larger stocks breeding across northern and eastern Europe and far into the USSR. These birds have to leave these areas in the autumn and great numbers of them fly south and west to winter in the same areas of Europe as the residents.

The Mute Swan has both sedentary and migratory elements to its population in north-west Europe, but in this case the two mostly remain separate. The birds of the British Isles, northern France and the Netherlands are sedentary, while the much larger numbers breeding in Scandinavia and eastern Europe are not. The latter move on to the Baltic for the winter, but unless the weather is very severe do not come further west than Denmark. Only in extreme conditions do small numbers reach the Netherlands, and the very south-east corner of England and there mix with resident birds.

One species, the Eider, is resident over most of its range, moving only very short distances up and down the coast. Those breeding in the high arctic islands of Spitsbergen and Franz Josef Land have to migrate, however, keeping south of the ice.

A number of species have quite short migrations, from inland breeding sites to the coast. For example, both the Red-breasted Merganser and the Goosander breed in northern Britain and Scandinavia and merely move to the nearest coast for the winter. Others of both species breeding further east in the USSR have to make rather longer journeys. The Harlequins of Iceland breed on rivers inland, and winter on sheltered coasts, often moving only a few tens of kilometres.

Wholly migratory species include the northern swans, though a few Whooper Swans do actually remain in Iceland while the rest leave for the British Isles, and all the arctic breeding geese. They may travel several thousand kilometres between summer and winter areas, often over the sea. Nearly all such populations also have migratory stop-over places, traditional haunts where they rest and feed for periods of days and weeks. Spring feeding places are of particular importance for the birds to put on weight prior to completing the migration and beginning to breed. Among the ducks, the Scaup, King Eider, and Smew completely vacate their breeding grounds. The Goldeneye, Common and Velvet Scoters are almost complete migrants, with tiny numbers breeding within the main wintering range.

In southern Europe and around the Mediterranean are some populations that are not highly migratory though all make some movements. For example the Marbled Teal seems to respond to periods of drought and rain more than the annual season, requiring as it does shallow water areas, which are often temporary. The White-headed Duck and Ruddy Shelduck of the western Mediterranean are probably mainly sedentary, or make at best short movements, but the birds of both species to the east do migrate more normally.

All of the species discussed so far move south or south and west in autumn with large numbers wintering within the region, though some, like the Pintail, may also move south of the Sahara. The Garganey is the exception to this pattern, as apart from a handful remaining around the Mediterranean for the winter, the whole population winters in the northern tropics of Africa.

Cold weather movements occur among many of the wildfowl species, especially those dependent on fresh water. In severe winters in western Europe, the majority of the Teal move further south and west, from Britain and the Netherlands, into western France and Iberia. On the few occasions when cold weather persists in the northern Mediterranean, the wintering birds there have moved to North Africa. Tufted Duck and Pochard also move out when freezing conditions occur in western Europe, but some species, like the Mallard, seem able to stick it out, perhaps moving to the coast, but not leaving their usual wintering range.

Mentioned briefly in connection with Canada Geese in Britain was a special type of movement called 'moult migration'. Typically it involves birds moving away from the breeding grounds to a special area where they will spend the period of the annual wing moult. In wildfowl all the flight feathers are shed simultaneously so that the birds are unable to fly until the new feathers have grown, a period of about three weeks in ducks, and up to five or six weeks for swans. Most other kinds of birds shed their wing feathers one or two at a time, waiting until new feathers are well grown before moulting any more. In this way the powers of flight are retained, though the period of moult is greatly prolonged. Wildfowl are able to adopt their strategy by virtue of being able to seek refuge on water when safety by flying is impossible, and being able to find all the food they require either in or very close to water.

Among the geese and swans, moult migrations are undertaken exclusively by non-breeders, immatures too young to breed, and by birds which may have tried to breed but which lost their eggs early on. Their moult migration typically takes them north of the breeding grounds to a separate area where they will stay from about mid-June to August, by when they are on the wing again. By going north they can make use of areas which are quite suitable for them, in terms of food and water, but which might not be usable for breeding. A snow-free period of three months is essential for most species of geese to complete their breeding cycle. In areas to the north of where they do breed there may be shorter snow-free periods which allow time for the moult but not for breeding. A major benefit to the population is gained if the non-breeding birds move away from the breeding area for most of the summer. The food resources of the breeding places are left entirely to the parent birds and their young, thus enabling the population to maximize its productivity.

Moult migration of this type has been found in Mute Swans in the Baltic, and in one or two areas in Britain, and in several parts of the ranges of Bean, Pinkfoot, Whitefront, Greylag, and Brent Geese. It also occurs, interestingly, in the introduced Canada Geese in Britain. It apparently lay dormant from the time they were introduced in the seventeenth century until about the 1950s, when small numbers of non-breeding and failed breeders were found to be migrating for the moult north from North Yorkshire to the Beauly Firth in Inverness. The habit has persisted and grown to the present 800–900 birds. Other populations of Canadas in Britain do not make moult migrations.

The Shelduck exhibits a complete type of moult migration. This involves almost all the adults in the whole north-west European population, breeders and non-breeders. The latter leave the breeding areas first, in June and early July, and move to the southern North Sea, to an area of shallow seas and extensive sand-banks rich in invertebrates in the Heligoland Bight. In July and August, as the young birds begin to grow, they amalgamate into large crèches of several broods, usually in the care of only one or two adults. The remainder of the parent birds then set off to the same moulting area. Once the moult is over the Shelducks make a slow movement back, some of them, such as the British population, return to their breeding range for the winter, others which breed further north and east to separate wintering areas.

Only male dabbling ducks perform a moult migration, which they do shortly after completing their share of the breeding chores, and the female is incubating the eggs. Mallard, Pintail, Teal, and Wigeon all move away to special moulting areas, often, though not invariably, somewhere along the line of the autumn migration, and pause there for the moult. After this is finished they complete their autumn migration to the winter quarters.

Tufted Duck, Pochard, and Red-crested Pochard have moult migrations like the dabbling ducks, though some adult females also take part, but not until their young are about half-grown, at which point they abandon them. Among the sea-ducks, eiders, scoters, and Goldeneye, most of which do not breed until they are two years old, have a moult migration performed by immatures as well as breeding males, taking them usually to sheltered areas of shallow sea, or sometimes large shallow lakes.

Food

Among the wildfowl of the West Palearctic are vegetarians, animal feeders, and omnivorous species. The larger birds, the swans and the geese, are almost entirely vegetarian, taking only small quantities of invertebrates, often perhaps inadvertently, as the animals cling to plants being eaten. The Shelduck is entirely an animal feeder, the dabbling and diving ducks more omnivorous, some taking more vegetable food than others, or in greater proportions at certain times of the year, or more animal food. The seaducks and sawbills are almost entirely animal feeders, eating insects, molluscs, crustaceans, and fish. Stiff-tailed ducks eat both insects and plants.

The feeding techniques of vegetable eaters include grazing, plucking, digging, and pecking. All the swans and geese graze at times, walking on dry land or in very shallow floods, pushing their partly opened bills into the vegetation. The bill is held slightly to one side and is then closed, trapping leaves and stems between the tooth-like lamellae on the sides of the upper and lower mandibles. The head is then jerked sharply backwards breaking off the fragments being held. These are pushed down the bird's oesophagous by the action of the tongue, aided by the rough projections on its surface. If the vegetation is short or very fine, the nail on the tip of the bill is used to grasp and clip off the pieces.

The typical grazers are the short-billed geese, the Barnacle, the Brent, and the Redbreast. All the other species do graze too but their heavier bills are also well adapted for other feeding techniques. Most grazing is on short grass and growing crops. Brent Geese traditionally feed on marine grasses and green algae on mudflats, though in recent years have taken to grazing on farmland too. Wigeon are the only duck to graze at all regularly, requiring quite short grass.

In thicker vegetation, and especially when feeding on plants underwater, the swans, geese and many dabbling ducks, pluck off the leaves and plants. This is done by a similar action to grazing but generally results in much larger pieces of food being broken off than when grazing on short pastures. Swans make use of their long necks to feed on bottom-rooted plants, up-ending if necessary. Most geese will also upend but not very commonly.

The swans and larger-billed geese regularly dig and probe for food items in soft mud, seeking roots and underground tubers of marsh plants. Greylags can be seen trampling with their feet among plants growing in shallow water, presumably trying to loosen and move away some of the mud from the roots. These same birds also eat potatoes and turnips in the fields, gouging out pieces with their bill nails, if they are too large to be swallowed whole.

Virtually all the swans, geese, and dabbling ducks make use of agricultural land for feeding at some time during the year, in particular gleaning spilt grains from harvested crops. Wheat, barley, maize, and beans are all taken, the grains being picked up one by one with a delicate pecking action. In some areas this taste for grain has extended to feeding on unharvested fields, often when the crop has been laid by wind and rain. Some geese have developed a seed-stripping technique, of grasping the head of corn between the mandibles and pulling sideways to remove the grains.

Dabbling ducks live up to their name by obtaining a great deal of their food from very shallow water, either swimming or walking with their bill just in the surface of the water, or dabbling at the edges where the maximum amount of food items may have been blown by the wind. All the dabbling ducks are omnivorous, taking seeds, insects, or plants depending on availability. As already mentioned Wigeon vary their diet through grazing. The Mallard has adapted to become an opportunist feeder, taking almost anything on offer, while the Shoveler, with its large spatulate bill and fine filtering mechanism down the sides, has the ability to sift finer items from the water surface than its relatives. Dabbling ducks extend their feeding range by upending, when the different lengths of neck will allow them varying opportunities and reduced competition, comparing say a Teal with a Pintail. They can dive for food but rarely indulge unless there is an unusual concentration on the bottom, as for example grain thrown into a waterfowl collection pond.

The true diving ducks usually submerge with a slight upward and forward jump. They do not use their wings underwater but solely their legs and feet. Plant leaves and stems are grasped and pulled off, or molluscs, crustaceans, and other invertebrates are seized in the tip of the bill. The smaller items are often swallowed underwater. The Red-crested Pochard and Ferruginous Duck are mainly vegetarians, the Pochard less so, at least when invertebrates are abundant. The Tufted Duck concentrates more on the invertebrates but is also known to take plants. Only the Scaup is mainly an animal feeder, and even it is an opportunist vegetarian, as for example when flocks gather round grain outfalls of breweries or distilleries.

Many of the sea-ducks, scoters, Long-tailed Duck, Harlequin, and goldeneyes, feed in the same way as the diving ducks. Most of the species feed to a considerable extent on molluscs which they are quite capable of prizing off a rocky bottom. They use their wings underwater to aid progress, and can dive to depths of several metres. The Longtail, in particular, regularly reaches 10 metres, perhaps much more, and stays down for up to a minute.

Two species of ducks feeding round the coasts have been studied in detail, and specialist feeding techniques have been described. The Shelduck eats a variety of small molluscs, insects, and crustaceans, obtained from shallow estuarine mud and sand. Its feeding techniques vary with the consistency of the mud, and the depth of water. When the surface is exposed, it may dig with its bill in hard mud, but when the mud is soft it adopts a side-to-side swinging action with its head and neck, scything the bill through the mud and thus locating the prey, as it slowly walks forward. This produces a very characteristic fern-leaf pattern in the mud.

In shallow water it will dip its head under, proceeding to upend as the water deepens. Foot-trampling is used to bring prey to the surface. These varying techniques enable the Shelduck to exploit different foods, and the maximum amount of time, within each tidal cycle.

The Eider Duck also eats molluscs, especially mussels, which it crushes in its powerful bill. The Shelduck seeks smaller items which are swallowed whole and then crushed in the gizzard. Eiders dive in anything from two to 15 metres of water, tearing the mussels off underwater rocks, or removing them from the bottom substrate. In shallow water they will do the same by upending or just by dipping the head below the surface. Another technique they adopt in such conditions is to sit rather upright in the water and then turn slowly round all the while kicking vigorously into the sand or mud with their feet. This produces a small crater into which the birds poke their bills as they turn, seeking food items.

Fish are eaten mainly by the sawbills, which are capable of swimming fast enough underwater to catch them, and have long bills with sharply serrated edges for grasping them. Like most fish-eating birds, they manipulate the fish in their bills so that they can swallow it head first.

The stiff-tailed ducks are accomplished divers and slip beneath the surface without any sort of a jump. The Ruddy Duck's feeding technique has been examined in detail and is probably followed by the White-headed Duck, and perhaps other species which feed on the bottom. It swims just above the bottom mud, with its head extended and bill tip just inserted into the mud. The bill is opened and closed in a rapid straining action while simultaneously the head and neck are swept from side to side.

The food and feeding techniques of wildfowl outlined above refer to adults and full grown young. The downy young of nearly all species feed at least initially on small insects, larvae, and very small seeds. They progress gradually towards a diet more like their parents'. All young wildfowl feed themselves, though in a few cases the parents may bring food within their reach. For example Mute Swans bring waterweed to the surface for their cygnets to feed on. Downy young of diving species are normally accomplished divers as soon as they leave the nest.

Social pattern and behaviour

Outside the breeding season wildfowl are gregarious birds, normally occuring in flocks, sometimes of only a handful of birds, but commonly up to many tens, and occasionally, hundreds of thousands. These flocks may cohere for long periods, or merely come together for short spells, perhaps at a particularly excellent feeding locality, or for night-time roosting. Roosts are frequently formed by birds flying in from several directions, flocks which have spent the day feeding in different areas. They join with other flocks for the night, but disperse again during the day. It is likely that despite the roost being formed of birds from very many flocks, some segregation is maintained, and discrete flocks reform as they leave the roost at dawn.

Within flocks there may be pairs and families, or groups of related immatures, the pattern varying with the species. The swans and geese all form pairs for life. This is a general rule, though with some exceptions. Among Mute Swans, for example, divorce and re-pairing by birds whose mates are still alive has been recorded in up to 6 per cent of pairs in one study area. Conversely among Bewick's Swans it has never been observed. A lasting pair bond in a migratory species, like the Bewick's Swan, is of greater importance than in a sedentary one, like the Mute Swan. This is because the family in swans and geese, more especially the migratory species, stays together throughout the first autumn and winter of the young birds' life. The parents literally lead their young on migration from the breeding grounds, showing by example where the migration stop-over localities and wintering places are. During the winter the young remain with their parents, being guarded by them. Because one of the parents, usually the male, is very watchful, the young can get on with feeding and continue to put on weight and to grow. Their survival is thus greater than if they also had to keep watch for danger.

The parent-young bond among sedentary Mute Swans is much less strong. The Mute Swan parents may go with their young into a wintering flock, but many pairs chase their young away in the autumn and the bond is severed. Young Mute Swans suffer considerably greater mortality through their first winter than young Whooper or Bewick's Swans.

The great majority of the ducks form pairs for a single breeding season. Pairing takes place through the winter or in the spring, and the birds separate again once the female has laid the clutch and begun incubating. The Mandarin Duck is an exception to this, as the pairs may stay together for several seasons. All the ducks are monogamous, taking just the one mate, but in several species, particularly the dabbling ducks, such as Mallard, and also in the Eider, the males may chase and rape other females.

The female duck incubates the eggs and brings up the young alone. Sometimes the male does stay with her after hatching, but this is exceptional, and normally the conspicuously-plumaged male does not associate with his family. The ducklings are reared by the female for varying lengths of time. In the dabbling ducks she looks after them until they can fly, or even after, while in some of the diving ducks, such as the Tufted Duck, she will abandon them while they are still only half-grown. Young stiff-tailed ducks are particularly independent and may separate from the adult female after only two weeks.

So far as is known, none of the ducks migrates in the autumn in family groups, the female having left her brood before this occurs. The young birds may travel in company with other young, and with adults, but no family bond is apparent.

The unusual system adopted by the Shelduck was mentioned in the Movements section. The young of several broods gather into crèches of up to 100 or so in the care of just a few adults, which are probably but not necessarily parents of young within the crèche. The remaining adults leave on their moult migration. Even the adults staying behind abandon the crèche of young before they have fledged. The pair bond in Shelduck, though, persists from year to year.

Some wildfowl, like the Barnacle and Brent Goose, and the Eider, nest in colonies for greater mutual protection. Others may form loose associations of nests, though not so regularly or closely spaced as to be termed colonies. Nearly all the ducks will nest close together on small islands in fertile lakes, but in other areas will nest far apart or singly. A few species are quite strongly territorial, driving off all others of their kind. This is particularly true of the swans, though interestingly the Mute Swan, normally highly territorial, will nest in colonies where the population becomes too great for the available territories.

Among some of the geese, both well dispersed and colonial breeding occurs; in the Pinkfoot, Greylag, and Canada, for example. The Bean Goose and Whitefront are widely spaced at all times, though without the birds actually defending a territory.

The Shelduck, once again, has a different pattern to other species. The pair first of all adopt a feeding territory on a section of mudflats, which they, or more especially the male, defend against other Shelduck. From here they fly inland to find a nest site. There is no territory defence here, indeed pairs may share a common opening to a multiple site, as in a hayrick. During the incubation period the male continues to defend the feeding territory, and the female visits it during her twice-daily spells off the nest. Once the young are hatched both parents lead them to a feeding area, which may or may not be the same as the original territory. In any case the family moves around, with the parents merely defending a flexible area around their broods, a system followed by geese. This period only lasts for some days before the Shelduck broods begin to amalgamate and the parents lose interest in their young.

Wildfowl have a wide variety of displays associated with courtship. In the most developed cases different displays are used for forming pairs, for maintaining them, and in the process of copulation. Variations on some of these displays, or further types of display, are used as a means of aggressive behaviour towards rivals, intruders, or potential predators. The full range of displays are far too many and too complicated to describe here. Instead brief summaries of the main types will be given.

Swans and geese have the least elaborate displays among the wildfowl of the region. Potential swan pairs face each other and then turn their heads from side to side. Geese have even less conspicuous movements; the female is courted by the male swimming ahead of her, with the tail cocked and the head held high. Both geese and swans reinforce and maintain the pair bond with the Triumph Ceremony. This is typically performed after the male has threatened or driven off an intruder. He returns to his mate calling loudly, in which she joins, the pair standing side by side,

often pointing their bills upwards. The wings are quivered at the same time, and sometimes the heads are moved up and down in a bowing action.

The birds with well-coloured plumage, the Shelduck, Mandarin, and dabbling ducks, make use of this colour, or their patterns, to enhance their various displays. Thus they may spread the wing to expose the colour pattern there, particularly on the shoulder or the speculum. The head plumes of the male Mandarin are shown to best advantage as the male turns his head while swimming round the female.

Dabbling ducks share a number of displays, with names that describe roughly what is going on, for example Head-up-tail-up, Grunt-whistle, Down-up, Burping, Preening-behind-the wing. Some of these, as the names imply, include calls. The female may respond with Inciting, in which she tries to persuade her selected mate to drive off others that may be continuing to court her. She points her bill at the offending bird and gives a low 'tock-tock' call. The less brightly coloured diving ducks have fewer and less elaborate displays, with names such as Kinked-neck, and Head-throw, as well as Turn-the-back-of-the-head.

Sea-ducks have a great variety of displays for pair-formation and maintenance, many of them designed to show off the brilliant black and white pattern of the males. Movements of the head are common, making the best use of the conspicuous markings on them. These include the bright yellow on the bill of the otherwise black Common Scoter, the red knob of the King Eider, the crest of the Red-breasted Merganser, or the shaggy head of the goldeneyes. Jerking the head low over the back, or throwing it forward with neck outstretched, are among the displays performed. Several species are quite vocal, including especially the cooing of the Eider, and the far-carrying three-note call of the Long-tailed Duck.

Another integral part of the pair formation of many duck species is the courtship flight. This is usually initiated by the female taking flight when she is being pressed by several males. One female may be followed by from two to as many as ten males, all of which try to stay as close to her as possible, calling repeatedly. The female herself may Incite whilst actually flying, indicating that one of the males may already have been selected as her mate, and that she would like him to rid her of the rest. These flights are frequent among Shelduck, dabbling, and freshwater diving ducks, and take place in the winter and spring.

A little later, and instead of courtship flights, the birds indulge in pursuit flights. These are more often of just three birds, and are often called 'three-bird flights'. They start when a strange male comes up to a mated pair of ducks and tries to force his attentions on the female. She may Incite her mate to drive off the intruding male but if this does not happen she may take flight, closely followed by the interloper and with her mate a little way behind. The female will probably Incite throughout the flight, which usually ends with the intruder abandoning his pursuit. Sometimes, however, he catches the female by the tail, forces her to the ground and then may copulate with her. Such 'rapes' are quite frequent among dabbling ducks, and also occur with diving ducks and Eiders. They are most frequent when incubating females come off the nest to feed and drink and no longer have their mate present to defend them. In these cases several males may pursue a female who makes desperate attempts to get away.

Normal copulation between a mated pair takes place several times in the period up to and during laying. In geese and swans it is initiated by the pair indulging in mutual Head-dipping, with the head going well under water. The display gradually rises in intensity until the male grasps the female at the back of the head and mounts her. Following copulation, wildfowl always carry out a further sequence of displays, which are thought to be important in reinforcing the pair-bond. In the case of the geese and swans they rise slightly out of the water, and call with head and neck stretched upwards, sometimes also opening their wings. Somewhat similar displays precede and follow copulation in shelducks and sheldgeese.

The dabbling ducks pump their heads up and down before copulation, rather than actually dip them in the water. Afterwards both male and female usually bathe. The Pochards dip their bills in the water and drink, before copulation; after it the female bathes while the male swims round her with his bill pointing steeply downwards.

In the sea-ducks the female takes up a prone position, with her head and neck lying along the surface of the water. The male then goes through a varied sequence of displays, usually similar to those used in courtship, together with some additional ones, such as drinking, and shaking the body plumage. After copulation the female bathes, while the male performs further courtship displays. The stiff-tailed duck males approach the female while flicking water from side to side with the tip of the bill. Afterwards the male displays, and the female bathes.

Breeding biology

Some of the behavioural and social aspects of wildfowl breeding were dealt with in the previous section, for example the duration of the pair-bond, the structure of the family, the presence or absence of territory, and its defence. This section will therefore concentrate on the more physical aspects of the subject.

Wildfowl in our area are all seasonal breeders, nesting only in the spring and summer. It is possible for the onset of the season to be brought forward a little or delayed by local conditions, such as rains or drought in the Mediterranean basin, or abandoned altogether, for example in very late springs in the arctic. In the south of the region the available time for breeding is several months, much longer than the time necessary to complete the breeding cycle. Thus in any given area individuals of the same species may start nesting over a considerable period, and there will be equal differences between species. In the far north the period suitable for breeding is only just long enough, and virtually all the wildfowl of whatever species will begin to lay within a matter of days. The average time for the onset of breeding in a species with a wide range, will, of course, vary with latitude, starting earlier in the south than in the north.

The majority of wildfowl nest on the ground, usually close to water. All three species of swans do so, the nest of the Whooper and Bewick's often being placed in marshy ground or on a small islet in a lake or river, as a defence against ground predators. Most geese nest on the ground in the open, though the Greylag breeds far enough south for it to be able to conceal its nest in tall marsh vegetation. Nests may be in colonies, or widely spaced, both giving some protection against predators, and frequently in marshy ground. In some parts of the arctic, the Barnacle Goose nests on inland cliff ledges, a hundred metres or more above the valley floor, and usually near the tops of scree slopes, providing a route down for the goslings. This is as a defence against arctic foxes. The Pink-footed Goose similarly chooses the tops of rocky outcrops and low cliffs. In its own, more vegetated habitat, the Greylag occasionally nests in the tops of pollarded willow trees.

Egyptian Geese normally nest on the ground in thick cover, but will also select cliff ledges, and occasionally holes. Both Shelduck and Ruddy Shelduck are predominantly hole nesters. Neither are capable of excavating their own hole or even enlarging one, but must adopt some already existing cavity. Rabbit holes in seawalls and dunes, holes under buildings, or in hay or straw ricks, are all favourites. The sole perching duck of the West Palearctic, the Mandarin, also nests in holes, almost invariably in trees, though also using nest-boxes.

Most dabbling ducks nest on the ground in thick vegetation. The site can be well away from water, a kilometre or more, though usually closer. The Mallard, in particular, will use trees, as well as less natural sites, including nest-boxes and cavities in buildings. Dabbling ducks are not colonial, but in protected sites, on favoured islands, for example, nests can be as close as a metre.

The pochards all nest in thick vegetation, either on the ground close to water, or actually in shallow water. Like the dabbling ducks, nests are normally well dispersed, but where protection is afforded, such as on islands, or when they nest in colonies of gulls, then they may be only a metre or two apart.

The eiders nest on the ground in the open, though in some southern breeding areas, they may become concealed as the surrounding vegetation grows. The Eider Duck is colonial, particularly where it is afforded special protection, and some colonies managed for their nest down in Iceland number thousands of pairs. The nests of all the eiders are usually placed fairly near water, but isolated nests some distance away are not unusual.

All the sea-ducks will nest in holes or cavities in the ground, but the Harlequin, Long-tailed Duck and the scoters, mainly nest in very thick vegetation, and rarely more than a few metres from the water. Barrow's Goldeneye in Iceland nest most frequently in lava and rocks, while the Goldeneye almost invariably chooses holes in trees. This habit has been used to advantage by erecting nest-boxes in woodland areas, whereby populations of Goldeneye have been greatly increased. The Smew similarly nests in tree-holes and will also use nest-boxes.

The Red-breasted Merganser and Goosander both nest in very well-concealed sites, including holes in river banks, among thick tree roots, or in dense clumps of heather or other plants. The Goosander sometimes nests up to a kilometre from the water, the Red-breasted Merganser usually closer.

Stiff-tailed ducks nest on low platforms of water vegetation floating in shallow water, in thick clumps of rushes. The White-headed Duck may sometimes build its own platform, but may take over the old nest of a Coot or other waterbird instead.

All the ground-nesting wildfowl build their nests from the nearest available vegetation. Most of the ducks first excavate a shallow cup by turning round and round, while pressing with their breasts and feet into the ground. None of the wildfowl can carry nesting material in their bills, and so nests have to be constructed with what they can reach while standing or sitting on the nest. Sometimes the male swan or goose, both of which help with the nest building, will stand a metre or two away and toss vegetation back over its shoulder bringing it within reach of the female on the nest. Some ducks make this material-tossing action when a short distance from the nest, but not very systematically and it is doubtful whether it adds much to the nest structure. In all duck species only the female builds. More material may be added by her during laying and incubation. The hole-nesting species make do without any nest material except what may happen to be present in the hole.

Once the laying of the eggs begins, the female will start to pluck down from her breast. She is only on the nest for a short period each day while laying, though staying longer and longer as the clutch becomes more complete. Thus the time spent down plucking also lengthens, and there will be a thick layer and rim of it by the time laying ends and incubation has begun. The swans produce only a very little down, but all the geese and ducks produce enough to line the nest and form a layer over the eggs, which is pulled into place when the incubating female leaves. This acts as insulation and to some extent camouflage. The down plumules of the different species are mostly distinguishable, while the presence of small breast feathers among the down makes identification certain. Thus used nests of ducks can be identified even though the owners have departed.

Wildfowl eggs are completely lacking in any spots, blotches, or streaks, so common among other birds' eggs. They are usually white, pale buff, olive, olive-green, pale green, or pale blue. Most swans and geese lay an egg every two days, but sometimes there is a gap of only 24 hours, particularly among the smaller geese. Ducks lay their eggs at one-day intervals, though in a large clutch there can be one or more gaps of two days. The number of eggs laid is variable, though within certain limits, among the different species. Those breeding in the far north tend to lay rather smaller clutches than those in the temperate regions, which have not had to undertake a long migration just before laying, and so have more food reserves to devote to the eggs. A large clutch also takes longer to lay, and time is not plentiful in the arctic summer. Whooper and Bewick's Swans normally lay between three and five eggs, but the average for Mute Swans in Britain is six. Northern geese usually lay between four and six eggs, while the Canada Geese and Greylags in western Europe can manage to lay five to nine. Similar variations will be found among the ducks. The largest clutch size is probably that of the Mallard, which in areas of abundant food supply can average as high as 12, though dropping to nine or ten in less favourable areas.

If the first clutch is successfully hatched, then the female will not lay further that season; all wildfowl are single-brooded in the West Palearctic. If the eggs are lost, particularly early on in the incubation period, then most species are capable of laying a replacement clutch, though this is usually smaller than the first one. Only the arctic breeding wildfowl do not relay. The breeding season is too short for a late-laid clutch to produce flying young before the onset of winter, and it is very rarely even attempted.

As soon as the clutch is complete the female starts full incubation. In no species does the male take part in incubation, though in a few, such as the swans, he may sit on the nest for short periods, for example before the clutch is complete or while the female is off the nest feeding. There have been recorded cases of male Mute Swans taking over the incubation after the death of the female, and successfully hatching the eggs, but only late on in incubation.

Wildfowl do not have a feather-free brood patch or patches as most other birds do. Instead the area from which the female has plucked her down acts as a brood patch, though it gradually grows new feathers while she incubates. The nest environment is usually a very damp one, but some degree of humidity is essential for the development and hatching of the egg.

The usual pattern of incubation is for the female to come off the nest once in the morning and again in the evening. She covers the eggs with nest material and down, and, among those species where the male stays with his mate through the summer, the pair move off to feed. In the case of the Shelduck this is to the special feeding territory, in other species it is to any suitable nearby area. The female may only be off the nest for perhaps half an hour and during this time will feed, bathe, and drink, while the male keeps guard, relieving her of this necessity. She can thus devote all her time to her own needs.

In species where the male has left the female, she may come off less than twice a day, and also less and less frequently as incubation proceeds. There are records of female Eider Ducks sitting throughout the entire 26–27-day incubation period, living on their reserves of fat and muscle.

The length of the incubation period varies from 21–22 days for the Teal and other small ducks to about 35 days for the Mute Swan. In general it is related to the size of the egg, but in the arctic the period is shorter than for similar sized eggs further south, which is another way in which the breeding season in the far north is compressed as much as possible.

All the eggs hatch more or less together, rarely spread over more than 24 hours. It usually takes about 48 hours for a chick to emerge from an egg, after the first star-shaped crack has appeared. The young bird can usually be heard tapping at the shell, and sometimes calling for a day or two before that. On hatching the down of the young wildfowl is covered in waxy sheaths and the birds are usually rather wet and slimy. The young are tired after the exertions of breaking out of the egg and generally sleep for several hours after hatching. During this period they dry out in the warmth under the female, and the waxy sheaths begin to rub off their down, leaving it fluffy and offering maximum insulation. After waking the youngsters become very active and restless, thus stimulating the female to lead them from the nest. They can walk or swim within six hours of hatching, though it is usually longer than this, 12 to 24 hours, before they actually do so. The timing of the exodus from the nest depends to some extent on time of day and weather, being delayed if it is dark, cold, or raining.

Birds nesting beside the water move straight on to it, but for some species there may be the preliminaries of leaving a nest hole, and a considerable walk. In the case of the Goldeneye, both may be involved. Young Goldeneye, and those of other hole-nesting species such as Mandarin and Smew, have strong claws and a very pronounced instinct to climb upwards towards light. This they do, from the bottom of their tree nest-hole, clinging on and jumping and scrambling out. They then free-fall to the ground, but as they are so light, and covered with down, they land quite softly. All this time the female is usually on the ground beneath the hole encouraging them with low calls. She then leads them to the water, which can, however, mean a trek of a kilometre or more. During this time ducklings can get lost and casualties occur. The reason for the birds nesting so far from water is probably related to a shortage of nest holes.

Both parents of the swans, geese, shelducks, and sheldgeese attend their young, keeping a watch for enemies, and defending them if necessary. Only the female does this in the case of the ducks. The young birds feed themselves right from the start, pecking innately at any small object and rapidly learning which represent food. While they are still small they are brooded by the female (or sometimes by the male in swans and geese), certainly every night, and also during any periods of rain. Later on they may huddle together for the extra warmth and protection this gives, though too large to fit under their parents, even when the latter spread their wings to accommodate them.

The smallest ducks fledge in about 25 to 30 days, the larger ones in 50 or 60. Some of the smaller geese, particularly those nesting in the arctic, manage to fledge in no more than 40–45 days, and the arctic nesting swans also have relatively short fledging periods, as an adaptation to the short summer of the region. The Mute Swan has the longest fledging period of any European wildfowl at about four months.

Plumages and moults

On hatching, all young wildfowl are completely covered in a soft downy plumage. Each down plumule has a centre shaft like a feather, with branches on each side. These, though, instead of being fairly stiff and interlocking to provide a degree of rigidity as in a feather, are long, soft, and free. This may well increase their insulating properties. The down is not naturally waterproof, though the down structure helps to repel water, as does a feather's. While the young are still being brooded, before they leave the nest, some of the female's waterproofing oil is transferred from her feathers to their down.

Some down plumules will be retained even after the young bird has fledged but most of it is pushed out by the feathers growing from underneath. The feathering starts as early as two weeks old in the smaller ducks, but not for four or five weeks in the swans. The process of feathering is constant in all the wildfowl, starting on the shoulders, breast, and belly. The head and neck are next, followed by the flanks and rest of the underparts. The last area of down is usually in the region of the lower back and rump. When the young bird is fairly well feathered, the wings and tail begin to grow. Another set of shorter down then grows under the feathers as an inner insulating layer. The main feathers and their cover grow nearly simultaneously. With the exception of the wing feathers, the down plumules are pushed out by the growing feathers, and in many areas remain as downy tips which then break off. The tail feathers of all wildfowl show a distinct notch in the tip where this occurred, and until the feathers are moulted this provides a wholly reliable ageing guide in those species where the juvenile and first year plumage is very similar to the adults', of great use to museum workers and those catching the birds for ringing.

The first full plumage is called juvenile and in all species a moult begins into an immature non-breeding plumage almost as soon as the birds have fledged. In some of the dabbling ducks and pochards, which will breed at one year old, this non-breeding plumage may actually only involve very few new feathers, and is rapidly and more or less completely overtaken by a moult into breeding plumage. This is very similar to that of the adult and can be detected only in the hand. This is possible for most species until about the New Year. The tail is almost always moulted during this phase but the wings never are.

In the slower-maturing species, the swans, the geese, and the sea-ducks, the juvenile plumage is more slowly and more completely replaced by an immature non-breeding dress. This may take the whole of the first year, and indeed may not be completed, so that some juvenile feathers are retained the full year.

In the first summer of the bird's life, it undergoes a complete moult, after the breeding season for those that have bred at one year old, or slightly earlier in the summer for the others. All the feathers are changed, including the wings, so that the bird becomes flightless for the first time. The birds which entered the moult in immature non-breeding plumage, moult into a more mature one, which may be fully adult, as in some of the sea-ducks, Shelduck and most geese, or may consist of a second immature non-breeding plumage, as in the swans, a few geese, and the eiders. The dabbling ducks and pochards, which were already in breeding dress, though not quite identical to the adults', moult first into eclipse plumage, a dull female-like dress, then shed the wing feathers, and only after regaining the powers of flight do they undergo a body moult once more, this time into full adult plumage.

Birds in second immature non-breeding plumage are capable of breeding at the end of their second year, while still wearing this dress, though many do not do so. They moult again in their second summer, and while in a few cases a third immature non-breeding plumage can be detected, in the Eider for example, to all intents and purposes, they are now in adult plumage. Some Whooper and Bewick's Swans retain grey flecking on the head and neck into their third or even fourth years, but there is much individual variation and others will be completely white at this age.

Adult shelducks, sheldgeese, and ducks all go through the sequence of a double body moult, one before and one after the moulting of their wing feathers. In the case of the brightly coloured males, this enables them to adopt a dull, well-camouflaged eclipse plumage for the period when they are flightless. However, the eclipse plumage of the Shelduck is only a little duller than the full black and white breeding plumage so the advantage here is not apparent.

Some of the dabbling duck females start moulting their body plumage into eclipse before they have started to lay their clutch, and complete it sometime after the eggs have hatched. Their eclipse plumage is hardly different from their breeding dress. Among pochards, however, the eclipse plumage of the females is a little duller than their breeding dress and this probably explains why these birds actually complete this first body moult before they start laying, and carry out their breeding duties in their eclipse plumage, after which they are ready to moult their wing feathers.

The most complex set of plumages and moults occurs in the Long-tailed Duck. It is difficult to fit it into the sequence and terminology used for other species, and various attempts to do so do not always agree with each other. Essentially both adult male and adult female have four plumages in the course of a year. The birds have a full winter plumage, worn from about November to early April, which is equivalent to breeding dress in other species. However, in the spring they perform a partial moult into a summer plumage, which is rather duller than the winter one, but in which they breed. Afterwards the moult continues until they are in full eclipse, during which the wings are moulted and the birds become flightless in the usual way. In about September they moult fairly completely into an autumn plumage, which is close to but not quite the same as their full winter plumage. This is attained by a further partial moult in about October–November. As in almost all other wildfowl the wings are moulted only once in the year, but some other feathers are shed and replaced no less than three times, most of the rest twice, but some of the body feathers, as well as the tail and wings, only once. The reasons for this curious pattern of moults and plumages are not clear.

The only known exception to the pattern of moulting the wing feathers just once in a year occurs in the Ruddy Duck. Here it seems that the wing feathers are replaced in the spring before the breeding season, as well as in the period afterwards. Thus the birds are flightless, for periods of about three weeks, twice each year. The body feathers are moulted at more or less the same time as the wings, so that the birds change from breeding to non-breeding plumage in the late summer, and back again to breeding plumage in the spring. There is no rapid double moult either side of the post-breeding wing moult as in other ducks. Thus the winter plumage, which is distinct from the summer plumage, is equivalent to an eclipse plumage.

The soft parts of wildfowl, their bills, legs, and feet, change colour as they mature, with the downy young and juveniles only rarely having any bright colours on these areas. Adults with coloured bills generally lose some of the intensity during the period of eclipse.

1 Mute Swan *Cygnus olor*
Whooper Swan *Cygnus cygnus*
Bewick's Swan *Cygnus columbianus*

The Mute Swan occurs on most types of wetlands throughout north-west and central Europe, with a population of about 120 000. Many thousands more are found in south-west and central USSR. They are resident in the milder areas; short distance migrants elsewhere. Mute Swans have been introduced into North America, Australia, New Zealand, and South Africa, though confined to a few localities.

The Whooper Swan breeds in Iceland, northern Scandinavia, and northern USSR, south of the tundra. The Iceland population of about 6000 birds winters mainly in the British Isles, a few remaining in Iceland. The continental population winters in north-west Europe (14 000 birds), south-west USSR (25 000), and the Far East. Winter habitat includes sheltered estuaries, lagoons, lakes, and marshes.

The Bewick's Swan breeds on the Siberian tundra. Two separate populations winter in north-west Europe (10 000 birds) and in the Far East. Mainly freshwater sites are used, or very sheltered estuaries.

The adult male and female Mute Swans (**1** and **2**) can be distinguished from the adult Whooper (**9**) and Bewick's (**10**) by their carriage, with the neck bent, the head pointing down, and the wings arched, and, at close range, by the red bill and black knob, larger in the male.

Distinguishing Whooper Swan from Bewick's Swan at a distance is always difficult, but the Whooper is not only larger, but has a proportionately longer neck and head. Closer to, the distinct difference in the amount of yellow on the bill of the adult becomes apparent. While both are variable, in the Whooper the yellow comes to a point on either side of the bill, extending beyond and below the nostril, halfway or more along the bill. The Bewick's yellow is truncated well before the nostril.

The adults of both species may show rusty staining on the head and neck (**10** and **15**), from ferrous salts in the water, though such staining is normally more frequent and more pronounced in the Whooper.

The juvenile Mute Swan (**4**) is brown not grey as in the Whooper Swan (**12**) and the Bewick's (**17**), and except for the Polish form, a genetic variant (**7**) with whitish plumage, lacks pink on the bill. All the young swans become whiter through the autumn. The immature Mute Swan (**3**) loses its remaining brown feathers in its first summer, retaining a few brownish feathers on the rump into its second year. Its grey bill gradually turns pink, while that of the Polish form is pink from the start. Second year Whooper (**11**) and Bewick's (**16**) retain some grey flecking on the head and neck, though their bills have attained adult colouring. This flecking can persist into the third or even fourth year and is not, therefore, a reliable ageing guide.

Downy young Mute Swans (**5**) are normally grey, though the Polish variety is white (**8**). The downy young of the Whooper (**13**) and Bewick's (**18**) are grey-white.

Mute Swans make a variety of snorting and hissing sounds, while their wings produce a musical throbbing in flight. Whoopers and Bewick's both have far-carrying bugle-like calls, but that of the Whooper is deeper and stronger.

Peter Scott.

Bean Goose *Anser fabalis*
Pink-footed Goose *Anser brachyrhynchus*
Greylag Goose *Anser anser*

There are several recognized races of the Bean Goose, two of which occur in Europe. The Western Bean *A. f. fabalis* breeds in the taiga zone of Scandinavia and USSR and winters on farmland and marshes in north-west and central Europe. The Russian Bean *A. f. rossicus* breeds on the Russian tundra and winters in north-west Europe, and further east in south-east Europe. Other races winter in China and Japan. The European winter population numbers at least 200 000.

The Pink-footed Goose is divided into two discrete populations breeding on the tundra of Iceland and east Greenland, and Spitsbergen. The former population numbers about 90 000 and winters on farmland in Scotland, and northern and eastern England. The latter, numbering about 15 000, winters on Dutch and Danish farmland.

The Greylag Goose has a scattered distribution, mainly in temperate marshlands, but also in low arctic scrub, from Iceland, northern Britain, and Scandinavia, east through central Europe and across Asia. The Iceland population of *c.*85 000 winters on farmland in Scotland, and Scandinavian and Russian birds winter in north-west Europe (20 000), southern and south-east Europe (80 000), and North Africa (6000). Further populations winter in Turkey, India, China, and south-east Asia. The birds of western Europe belong to the Western race *A. a. anser*, the remainder are Eastern Greylags *A. a. rubrirostris*.

The male and female of each of the three species are alike. The adult Western Bean Goose (1) is distinguished by its dark brown head and longish neck, and the general brown tone of the rest of its plumage. There is an orange band over the top of the black bill and orange along the sides. This is very variable and birds can have completely orange bills (2), occasionally with some white feathering at the base. The bill is elongated and thus distinct from the shorter, stouter bill of the Russian Bean Goose (5) which additionally has the orange confined to a band over the top. Apart from the Russian Bean's smaller and rounder head and smaller size, the two races are very similar.

The adult Pink-footed Goose (6) is a little smaller than the Bean Goose and is greyer overall. Its dark head is rounder and its neck shorter. The bill has a pink stripe over the top and the legs are also pink not orange. The bill can have more extensive pink (7), with occasionally white feathering at the base.

The Western Greylag (10) is generally grey, lacks a dark head, and has a stout orange bill. The Eastern Greylag (13) is larger and paler and has a pink bill. The Greylag's head is larger in proportion to its body than the other species. The black belly markings on the adults are never as heavy as on the White-fronted Goose *A. albifrons*.

The first-winter birds of all three species (3: Bean; 8: Pinkfoot; 11: Greylag) can be told from their adults by the lack of regular pale feather edgings on the wing coverts, and also by the slightly mottled chest and belly. The bill and leg colour is also duller than the adults'.

The Bean Goose downy young (4) is olive-green above, while the Pinkfoot (9) tends to be more yellow, though this bleaches quite quickly. Greylag young (12) are similar to those of the Bean Goose though young of the Eastern race (14) are rather yellower and paler.

3 White-fronted Goose *Anser albifrons*
Lesser White-fronted Goose *Anser erythropus*

Two races of White-fronted Goose occur in Europe, and a further two or three in North America. The European Whitefront *A. a. albifrons* breeds on the tundra of Eurasia, the western birds migrating to winter on farmland and marshes from north-west Europe to the Middle East, the more easterly birds wintering in China and Japan. The European birds are divisible into several more or less discrete populations totalling perhaps half a million, of which 200 000 can be found in north-west Europe. It has increased here very considerably in recent years.

The Greenland Whitefront *A. albifrons flavirostris* breeds on wet tundra and heathland in West Greenland and winters on bogs and farmland in western Britain and Ireland. It has a small population of about 15 000 and has declined over the last few decades through reclamation of its winter habitat. The North American races winter in the Pacific and Gulf states of America and in Mexico.

The Lesser Whitefront breeds in a narrow belt of semiwooded tundra from northern Scandinavia across Eurasia to the Pacific. About 5000 birds from the western part of the range winter in marshes and farmland in southern and south-east Europe, and the Middle East; the eastern breeders winter in the Far East. Stragglers occur every winter in north-west Europe. This species has decreased in numbers in the last 30 years, at least in the western part of its range.

The adults of all the Whitefronts show a combination of a prominent white forehead and black belly bars on their overall brown plumage. The barring is very variable and can be used to identify individuals at close range. Adult Greenland Whitefronts (**1** and **2**) have the least white on the forehead and an orange bill. The general tone of the Greenland Whitefront's plumage is much darker than that of the European Whitefront adults (**5** and **6**) which also show much more white, and have a pink bill.

The immatures of both races (**3**: European; **7**: Greenland) do not obtain the white forehead until well into the winter, while the black belly bars rarely if ever appear before their second year. As in other grey geese the wing coverts of the immatures lack the regular pale barring of the adults, and the underparts are slightly mottled. The colour of the bill and legs is duller than in the adults.

The adult Lesser Whitefront (**9** and **10**) is a dainty bird in comparison with the larger Whitefronts, having a smaller rounded head and a much shorter, steeper bill, which is also quite a bright pink. The white forehead extends on to the top of the head. At close range the yellow eyering and the fact that the closed wings extend beyond the tip of the tail help to distinguish this species, as does its rapid gait. The belly barring is variable. The immature Lesser Whitefront (**11**) resembles a small immature European Whitefront, except for the shape of the bill, and the presence of the yellow eyering.

The downy young of Whitefronts (**4**: European; **8**: Greenland) and Lesser Whitefronts (**12**) are similar, being olive brown above and yellowish below.

Whitefronts have a high-pitched laughing call, while the Lesser Whitefront's is a more squeaky version of this.

Canada Goose *Branta canadensis*
Barnacle Goose *Branta leucopsis*

Canada Geese are native to North America where about 12 subspecies are currently recognized. Introduced birds are fully established in Britain (*c*.25 000) and Sweden (*c*.10 000), with small numbers in Norway, Finland, and West Germany. Those in Britain are mainly resident; at least some Swedish birds move south in winter. The birds live on all types of fresh water, feeding on adjacent farmland.

There are three discrete populations of Barnacle Geese breeding on high arctic coasts and wintering in north-west Europe. Here they roost on estuarine mudflats and sheltered sea lochs, feeding principally on improved grassland and stubbles, though formerly restricted to grazed saltmarsh and grassy islands. About 30 000 breed in east Greenland and winter on islands of western Scotland and Ireland. The smallest population (9000) breeds in Spitsbergen and winters in the Solway Firth (Scotland/England border). About 50 000 breed in north-west USSR and winter in the Netherlands.

Virtually all the introduced Canada Geese in Europe belong to the nominate race *canadensis*. The adult (**1**) shows a sharp demarcation between the black neck stocking and the pale chest. Some large specimens have been attributed to the race *maxima* (**4**) which often shows a little more white on the head. Canada Geese of several other races are widely kept in captivity and escapes, or possibly genuine wild vagrants, may turn up almost anywhere. The commonest are: *interior* (**5**), about the same size as *canadensis* but darker on the underparts and so lacking the same sharp boundary at the base of the neck; *taverneri* (**6** and **7**), which is smaller than *canadensis*, also fairly dark on the breast and sometimes with a white ring at the base of the neck; *minima* (**8** and **9**), which is much smaller and darker, the neck stocking sometimes merging with the breast, though occasionally divided by a narrow white collar; and *hutchinsii* (**10**), almost as small as *minima* but with a pale breast. Caution is urged against field identification of most of these races as intergrades occur.

The adult Barnacle Goose has the whole face white (**11**) or sometimes creamy (**12**), with the white extending across the forehead, in contrast to the 'chin-strap' of the Canada Goose. The black neck extends down to cover the chest as well. At a distance the overall impression is of a compact black, white, and silvery-grey goose. The immature (**13**) has a dull and very slightly mottled neck and chest, and brown edgings to the flank feathers. The wing coverts additionally lack the white edgings and the effect of parallel barring found in the adult, giving the bird a duller, browner appearance. The downy young (**14**) is distinctively medium grey above and white below.

The call of the Canada Goose is a deep and resonant honking, while the Barnacle Geese have a shrill barking call which, when coming from a flock, sounds rather like a pack of yelping dogs.

The smallest races of Canada Geese are similar in size to Barnacle Geese but overall brown in colour not black and grey, so confusion at a distance should be slight.

5 **Brent Goose** *Branta bernicla*
Red-breasted Goose *Branta ruficollis*

Brent Geese of three distinct races have a circumpolar distribution on coastal tundra and small islands in the high arctic. Wintering habitat was formerly confined to estuarine mudflats where the birds fed on eelgrass *Zostera* and algae *Enteromorpha* and *Ulva*. In recent years feeding has developed on grassland and arable fields adjacent to the coast. Dark-bellied Brent Geese *B. b. bernicla* from Siberia winter on the coasts of north-west Europe. They have increased from 30 000 in the mid-1960s to over 150 000. Some 2–3000 Light-bellied Brent *B. b. hrota* breeding in Spitsbergen and Franz Josef Land winter in Denmark and northern England. Another population of *c.*9000 come from north-east Canada and northern Greenland to winter in Ireland. Yet others from arctic Canada winter in eastern USA. Black Brant *B. b. nigricans* breed in north-west Canada, Alaska, and north-east USSR and winter in California and Mexico. Stragglers occasionally reach Europe.

Red-breasted Geese breed in open or slightly wooded tundra in northern Siberia. They winter in the Balkans and around the Caspian. The population has decreased sharply since the 1950s to the present *c.*20 000.

Brent Geese are small short-necked geese. The adult Light-bellied Brent (**1**) shows a sharp boundary between the black chest and the whitish belly. The adult Dark-bellied Brent (**5**) has little or no demarcation here, the belly being dark grey, shading paler towards the rear. Vagrant Black Brant (**9**) can be distinguished by the broad whitish flanks, always more conspicuous than in the Dark-bellied race, and by the white neck ring, which is complete round the front of the neck instead of being split into a separate white blaze on each side, as in both Light-bellied and Dark-bellied Brent.

Juvenile Light-bellied Brent (**3**) moult gradually in the early autumn into first-year plumage (**2**) with the white neck markings appearing in the New Year. In contrast to other geese it is the immature which has distinct pale edgings to the wing coverts, and these are retained through the first winter. The adult's closed wings show little or no pattern. The Dark-bellied Brent is similar with the juvenile (**7**) and immature (**8**) staying quite distinct from the adult on the wings, and with the white neck mark appearing during the winter. The downy young of all races (**4**) is grey-brown above, pale grey below.

Adult Red-breasted Geese (**10**) are very boldly patterned, though curiously the dark-red neck and breast and well marked head are not easy to see at a distance. More conspicuous is the bold white flank mark. Immature Redbreasts (**11**) are less clearly marked than the adults, and the white edgings to the wing coverts are duller and less regular. A few birds at this age may lack the red cheek patch (**12**). The overall colour of the downy young (**13**) is greenish brown, paler below.

Brent Geese have a distinctive 'rott rott rott' call, which is far-carrying and somewhat metallic in tone. Red-breasted Geese have a shrill double call, 'kee-kwa'.

Peter Scott.

6 Snow Goose *Anser caerulescens*

Snow Geese of two races breed from north-west Greenland right across arctic Canada and Alaska and into the north-eastern part of the USSR. Very small numbers of Greater Snow Geese *A. c. atlanticus* breed in north-west Greenland with the vast majority on lowland tundra in north-eastern Canada. They winter on farmland and marshes in eastern USA. They have increased from around 40 000 in the mid-1950s to over 200 000.

Lesser Snow Geese *A. c. caerulescens* breed in central northern and north-western Canada, in Alaska, and on Wrangel Island, USSR. About two million birds from Canada winter around the Gulf of Mexico. Those from more westerly colonies winter in the Pacific coast states of the USA and in western Mexico, and number about half a million.

The status of the Snow Goose in Europe is obscured by the fact that it is widely kept in captivity, and full-winged specimens are frequent. Escapes are common, even in small flocks of up to 20. Genuinely wild vagrants of either race may be occurring, particularly perhaps in flocks of Greenland White-fronted Geese *A. albifrons flavirostris* in western Britain and Ireland, but even here escapes from captivity may turn up. There has recently been a sighting in the Netherlands of a bird marked in North America; the first confirmed transatlantic vagrant.

The Lesser Snow Goose occurs in two main colour phases, white and blue, though there are five recognizable intermediate phases, while the Greater Snow Goose is always white. Differences between the adult Greater Snow (1) and the adult white phase Lesser Snow (3) are slight. The former is rather larger and bulkier, but this is really only useful when comparisons can be made. The Greater Snow's bill is longer and heavier, and there is a much more conspicuous 'grinning patch', the gap between the upper and lower mandibles. Certain separation in the field is very difficult. The blue phase Lesser Snow Goose is unlike any other goose, with the very prominent white head and upper neck set on a dark grey body. The bill and legs are the same pink as in the white phase. The intermediate forms between the blue and white phases usually show the same upperparts colour but have varying amounts of white on the belly and chest.

Immature Greater Snow Geese (2) and white phase Lesser Snow Geese (4) are very lightly washed and speckled grey-brown, with duller bill and legs. The only distinctions between them are size and the shape of the bill, as in the adult. The immature blue phase Lesser Snow (6) is very dark grey all over, except for a little white under the chin of some birds, and on the undertail coverts. A few white feathers may appear on the head and neck before the end of the winter. Brown edgings to the wing coverts and flank feathers give the bird a duller appearance than the adult.

Snow Geese of both races have a rather harsh cackling call, together with some honking notes.

Peter Scott

7 Egyptian Goose *Alopochen aegyptiacus*

The Egyptian Goose is found over virtually the whole of Africa south of the Sahara, only penetrating north of it down the Nile valley into southern Egypt. Its habitat is inland fresh water, running or still, with an abundance of vegetation. Stragglers winter in the Middle East and North Africa, and it is reported to have formerly bred in both areas, as well as in the Danube valley in Hungary 2–300 years ago. There is a small resident population of a few hundred birds in eastern England, mainly Norfolk. Records from elsewhere in Europe are probably of escapes from captivity.

Egyptian Geese are long-legged rather upright birds. There are two colour forms of the adult, the rufous (1) and the grey (2). The names refer to the colour of the mantle and scapulars; in all other respects the two forms appear identical. Some intermediate forms may occur. The pale head with the dark eyepatch is very distinctive, though the dark breast patch is less obvious. If the wings are drooped even slightly the vivid white of the forewing is immediately apparent. The immature bird (3) is much duller and paler than the adult and lacks both the dark eyepatch and breast mark. It has a distinct capped appearance from the darker crown and back of the neck, running down to the brown upperparts. The downy young (4) has prominent white markings above the eye and on the back and wings. The female Egyptian Goose has a harsh trumpeting call, but the male's vocabulary is restricted to rather laboured, gusty breathing sounds.

8 Ruddy Shelduck *Tadorna ferruginea*

The Ruddy Shelduck breeds in Greece, the Balkans, Turkey, Iran, through southern USSR, and into China. There is a small isolated stock in southern Morocco estimated to include 1–2000 breeding pairs. Altogether in the Mediterranean and Black Sea areas there are thought to be about 20 000 birds. Decreases have been noted from most parts of the range. Vagrants have occurred in most European countries, though some may have been escapes from captivity. Although not usually found on maritime coasts, Ruddy Shelduck live in shallow saline waters, around salt lakes and inland seas, as well as in most types of freshwater habitat.

Adult male (1) and female (2) Ruddy Shelduck differ only slightly. The male is more orange and less chestnut, and so paler overall, and has a narrow black collar, lacking in the female. Both sexes are somewhat variable in the amount of creamy white on the face, though the female usually has more white there, and also on the wing coverts. The only possibility of confusion is with the Cape Shelduck *T. cana,* an occasional escape from captivity, which has a grey or grey and white head and more contrast between upper- and underparts. Outside the breeding season the male Ruddy Shelduck (3) usually loses his black collar.

The immature is duller and browner than the adult, particularly on the head and back. The downy young's most distinctive features (5) are the white spots on the back.

Ruddy Shelducks have loud and penetrating trumpet-like calls.

9 Shelduck *Tadorna tadorna*

Shelduck occur widely round the coasts of north-west Europe, and locally in the western Mediterranean, the Balkans, southern USSR, China, and Mongolia. Some populations are resident, but migrants reach North Africa, India, and southern China. The north-west European population is estimated at 130 000 birds, that in the Mediterranean and Black Seas at about 75 000. Shelduck are restricted to the coast or to inland salt seas, only occasionally occurring on freshwater.

The bold patterning of the adult Shelduck is essentially similar in both male (1) and female (2). The goose-like shape, and mainly white plumage, contrasting with the dark green, chestnut and black, plus the red bill and pink legs, are quite unmistakable. The female has a paler bill with a reduced knob compared with the male, while the coloured parts of her plumage are generally a little duller. There may be some white flecking round the base of the bill. The male has a post-breeding eclipse plumage (3) in which his pattern becomes much less clear-cut, with white mottling around the face, and on the breast band and belly stripe.

The juvenile Shelduck (5) is grey-brown above and pure white beneath, with much white on the face. During the autumn this plumage moults to an immature state (4) which is a duller version of the adult's with white flecking in the coloured areas. The downy young (6) shows rather more white on it than the young Ruddy Shelduck *T. ferruginea*.

Male Shelduck have musical whistling calls, while the female makes deeper chattering quacks.

10 Mandarin *Aix galericulata*

The natural range of the Mandarin lies in Japan, north-eastern China, and extreme western USSR. Some winter in eastern China and Korea. Within Europe there is a small resident population of several hundred birds in south-east England, with small numbers locally elsewhere including Scotland. In the Far East Mandarins live by lakes, pools, and slow-moving rivers containing some emergent vegetation, and bounded by mature trees. In Britain, they occur in well-wooded parkland containing lakes, and alongside rivers. The need for nest-sites in hollow trees, stumps, etc., may be restricting its expansion in Britain, despite its frequency in captivity and many escapes. The latter have provided scattered records from many European countries.

The adult male (1) is quite unmistakable with its remarkable 'sails', actually greatly enlarged inner flight feathers. The adult female (2) and immature (4) are also not like any other European duck, though difficult to distinguish from the North American Wood Duck *A. sponsa* which is common in captivity and may be becoming established in the wild in a few places. The Wood Duck is more green above and has a larger patch of white round the eye, lacking the rear-pointing stripe leading from it. From about June to October the male is in an eclipse plumage (3), becoming much like the female, but retaining his pink bill, more colour to his plumage, and a thicker crest. The downy young Mandarin (5) closely resembles the young of dabbling ducks *Anas* though not so yellow as most of these.

The male Mandarin has a sharply rising whistling call, while the female mostly gives a single sharp 'kett'.

Many observations of geese in flight are at great range or in poor light, so that colour and even pattern barely show. Emphasis is therefore given here on shape as well as colour.

Bean Geese (**1**) are long-winged, long-necked birds, rather evenly dark all over, but showing a darker head and neck close to.

Pinkfeet (**2**) are shorter in the neck than other grey geese, and have a small rounded head. At closer range the grey tones on the upper wing become visible.

Western Greylags (**3**:adult; **4**:immature) have stout necks and noticeably large heads and bills. The pale grey forewings are often conspicuous even at considerable distances. The wings are rather broad and short. Eastern Greylags (**5**) also show the pale forewing, and an even larger head and bill.

Greenland Whitefronts (**6**:adult; **7**:immature) have long dark wings, and the adults look very dark underneath. The white forehead hardly shows at a distance. The immatures are paler underneath but with evenly dark wings.

European Whitefronts (**8**:adult; **9**:immature) are also long-winged but not as dark. The white forehead is more obvious, and the immature is much paler underneath.

Lesser Whitefronts (**10**:adult; **11**:immature) are small and agile in flight, with a relatively short neck and round head. The white forehead is quite conspicuous. The immature lacks any obvious markings.

Adult white phase Lesser Snow Geese (**12**) are unmistakable with their white body and black primaries. The immature (**13**) is very pale with darker wings.

The white head and neck and dark body immediately distinguish the adult blue phase Lesser Snow (**15**). The rare intermediate form (**14**) is also unmistakable. The immature blue phase (**16**) can be readily confused with a young Whitefront

which, however, is longer-winged and shows white on the tail.

Brent Geese are very short-winged, short-necked geese. Light-bellied Brent (**17**:adult; **18**:immature) are readily distinguishable by their underpart colour from Dark-bellied (**19**:adult; **20**:immature), but the immatures can barely be separated from the adults except at very close range.

Barnacle Geese (**21**) show black and white in flight, except at extreme distances, while their silhouette is of a relatively short-necked goose with well pointed wings.

Canada Geese are dark-winged birds with black necks. The white face patch may not show well in flight. Their proportions vary according to race. The large, pale birds resident in Britain and other parts of Europe (**22**) have very long, thin necks, the black contrasting with the paler breast and belly. Smaller races, true vagrants or escapes from captivity, have shorter necks and may be dark underneath (**23**) or pale (**25**), while either kind may have a thin white neck ring at the base of the black stocking (**24, 26**).

The white wing bars on Red-breasted Geese (**27**:adult; **28**:immature) barely show in flight, though the patterned head and neck does. The neck looks short; the wings pointed.

Egyptian Geese (**29**:adult; **30**:immature) flash their bold white forewings in flight, visible at great distances. Their silhouette is very goose-like with the long neck and wings.

Shelducks (**31**:adult; **32**:immature) look black and white at any distance, and more like a goose than a duck, though their flight tends to be rather deliberate.

Although the Ruddy Shelduck (**33**) has a white forewing like the Egyptian Goose, it lacks the long neck and pale underparts of that species, and its flight is more duck-like.

Peter Scott.

12 Wigeon   *Anas penelope*

The Wigeon breeds in thick cover near lowland wetlands throughout the boreal and subarctic zones of Eurasia, including Iceland, northern Britain, and from Scandinavia to the Pacific coast of the USSR. Wintering grounds lie to the south, in north-west Europe, around the Mediterranean and Black Seas, in East Africa, the Middle East, India, south-east Asia, China, and Japan. About one and a half million birds are thought to winter in Europe and western Asia, mainly in estuaries and shallow coastal lagoons, but also on some inland flooded grasslands.

The pale forehead on the chestnut head of the adult male (1) with the grey back and flanks, and the white forewings which show at rest, combine to make it easily identifiable from any other duck, except perhaps American Wigeon (q.v.). The adult female (2) can be distinguished from other female dabbling ducks by her overall rufous tinge, white belly and steep forehead. The eclipse male (3) is superficially like the adult female but is more rufous, darker on the upperparts, and still shows white from the forewings. This plumage lasts from July to about November.

Immature Wigeon (4) closely resemble the adult female and are doubtfully distinguishable in the field, especially as young males do not get any white on their wings until their second year. The downy young (5) has the typical *Anas* pattern but with a much reduced eyestripe, which is merely a streak; the face is also rather reddish.

The male Wigeon has a distinctive two-note whistling call; the female a low purring growl.

13 American Wigeon   *Anas americana*

This species replaces the Wigeon *Anas penelope* in North America, breeding in similar habitat from eastern Canada (locally) westwards to Alaska. It winters on all coasts of USA and Mexico. Stragglers reach Iceland, Britain, and Ireland fairly regularly, and are occasional elsewhere in western Europe.

Although the adult American Wigeon (1) has a superficial resemblance to the Wigeon, with its prominent pale forehead, the head pattern when seen well is quite different. The dark green eyepatch on the whitish head is very distinctive. The effect is of a pale head on a darker body, the opposite of the Wigeon.

The adult female American Wigeon (2) is extremely like the female Wigeon but can be identified on a plumage difference that has been noticed since the plate was painted. The tertials of the American Wigeon have pure white margins and black centres, showing as three or four narrow parallel bars. The female Wigeon's tertials are dull brown and the margins are buff to off-white, showing as indistinct barring at best.

The eclipse male (4) resembles the adult female but shows white along the side from the forewing, even when the wing is closed. It is also richer in colour than the female. The immature male by mid-winter (3) looks very like the adult but lacks the white forewing.

The whistling call of the male American Wigeon is rather similar to that of the Wigeon but has three notes not two. The female sounds like the female Wigeon.

14 Falcated Duck *Anas falcata*

Most records of this species in Europe probably refer to escapes from captivity but occurrences in Turkey, Jordan, and Iraq are thought to have been genuine vagrants. The Falcated Duck breeds beside rivers and lakes in forested regions of eastern Siberia and Mongolia, and winters in China, Japan and south to Burma.

The adult male (1) should be immediately identified by its very large-looking head with its considerable mane of purple and bronze-green feathers. The rear end, too, has an odd shape from the long black, grey, and white scapulars drooping over the tail. The overall effect is of a very squat large-headed duck, very pale bodied, but with dark head and tail.

The adult female (2) most resembles the female Gadwall *Anas strepera* but is rather browner and darker, less grey-brown. If the underparts can be seen these are mottled brown all over, compared with the white of the Gadwall. Closer to, the Falcated Duck has a relatively large head, gained from the slight crest, while the bill is dark grey or black. The female Gadwall has a brown bill with orange along the sides. Finally if the speculum shows the Falcated Duck's is green and black, lacking any of the white shown by the female Gadwall.

The immature Falcated Duck (3) closely resembles the adult female though the crown and upperparts are a little darker. Males do not attain full plumage until the late winter.

The male has a low trill; the female quacks like a Gadwall.

15 Gadwall *Anas strepera*

The Gadwall has a wide distribution, breeding beside fresh waters in open lowlands, locally throughout Europe, and across the western half of USSR, and the western part of USA. It winters mainly to the south of this range on shallow fresh waters as well as estuaries. About 10 000 winter in north-west Europe, with a further 50 000 in the Mediterranean–Black Sea region. The species has increased and spread in Europe this century.

The adult male (1) is a predominantly grey duck, the same shape as a Mallard *A. platyrhynchos* but a little smaller. The black under the tail has no white immediately in front of it, as in Mallard, Wigeon *A. penelope* and Pintail *A. acuta*. The dark grey bill is much finer than the Mallard's and the forehead a little steeper. White from the speculum shows if the wing is spread.

The adult female (2) is very like the female Mallard but has a thinner bill and steeper forehead. The white speculum is a good feature if it shows. Out of the water the female Gadwall has white underparts, the Mallard brown.

In eclipse the male (3) becomes like a dark female, retaining his chestnut wing coverts.

As in most ducks the juvenile (5) is like the adult female, but with brown underparts, thus very similar to a Mallard, though greyer. By December young males (4) are looking like adults though keeping most of the juvenile wing.

The downy young is similar to that of Mallard but paler.

The male Gadwall has a weak, nasal croak, the female a soft quack.

16 Teal *Anas crecca*

The smallest of the dabbling ducks, the Teal breeds from the arctic tundra south almost to the desert regions in Eurasia and North America. On the latter continent the nominate *crecca* is replaced by the American Green-winged Teal *A. c. carolinensis*. Wintering mainly to the south of the breeding range the habitat includes estuaries, coastal lagoons, floods and large reservoirs. The population of north-west Europe has been estimated at 150 000, while perhaps three-quarters of a million winter in the Mediterranean–Black Sea area. *A. c. carolinensis* is an almost annual straggler to Britain and Ireland, with rare occurrences elsewhere in Europe.

The very small size distinguishes the Teal from almost all other European ducks. At a distance the adult male (1) shows a dark head and pale body, while close to the head pattern is very distinctive. While the male *crecca* has a white stripe along the flank, the male *carolinensis* (6) has a vertical white stripe just behind the breast which is completely diagnostic. Female and immature *carolinensis* cannot be distinguished from *crecca*.

The adult female (2) is small, brown and unmarked, apart from a pale eyestripe visible at close range. The eclipse male (3) is similar but darker with fewer buff edgings. The juvenile (5) is also like the adult female but has brown spotting on the lower breast and belly. The downy young (5) has the usual *Anas* pattern but with a second dark stripe below the eye.

The male Teal has a very distinctive musical double whistle, while the female makes a high-pitched quacking.

17 Cape Teal *Anas capensis*
Marbled Teal *Marmaronetta angustirostris*

The Cape Teal is found on fresh and brackish water over a wide area of eastern and southern Africa. There have been a handful of records from the West Palearctic, including two pairs seen displaying in Libya, and so perhaps nesting.

The Marbled Teal has a scattered breeding distribution in Spain and western North Africa, Turkey, the Middle East, Iran, and southern USSR. Some birds are resident, others move south, across the Sahara, into Egypt, Iran, and northern India. Most freshwater habitats are used within its range. Numbers in Spain have declined seriously this century to under 100 pairs; some hundreds of pairs breed in North Africa. Several thousand birds winter in Iran.

The adult Cape Teal (1) is readily identified by its pale spotted plumage and pink bill. The immature (2) is a little duller with a darker bill. The only possible confusion could be with Marbled Teal.

The adult male Marbled Teal (3) is more cream and brown than the Cape Teal, less grey, has a dark bill, a conspicuous dark eyepatch, and a shaggy back to the head. The adult female (4) generally lacks this last feature but is otherwise identical to the male. The immature (5) resembles the adult but is duller and greyer on the upperparts, lacking many of the creamy spots on the back and flanks. The downy young has a washed out plumage though of the basic *Anas* pattern.

Neither species calls much. The male Cape Teal has a soft whistle and the male Marbled Teal a low croak. Both females make subdued quacks.

18 Mallard *Anas platyrhynchos*

The Mallard breeds throughout Europe and across Asia to northern China and Japan, though avoiding the arctic regions. It also occurs in most of northern North America, except the north-east. Many are resident; others winter to the south of the breeding range. Mallard have adapted to the widest possible range of wetland habitat available to them, for breeding and wintering. This is easily the most numerous wildfowl in Europe with an estimated one and a half million wintering in north-west Europe and a similar number in the Mediterranean–Black Sea region.

The adult male (1) can be regarded as totally familiar and unmistakable, with its dark green head, white collar, chestnut breast and grey flanks. The adult female (2) is unremarkable when at rest, with a slightly darker cap to her head, and a dark line through the eye the only features.

The eclipse male (3) is greyer than the female, and has a more pronounced dark cap, a warmer brown breast, and a yellow bill. The immature (4) is also female-like, though more streaked and less spotted on the flanks and underparts. Males become recognizable as early as September as they acquire adult plumage. The downy young (5) has a distinct line through the eye and a small dark spot below and behind it.

Male Mallard make a soft 'quek' call, while the female has the very familiar range of quacks, including the decrescendo call of several notes strung together.

19 Black Duck *Anas rubripes*

The Black Duck breeds in Eastern North America wintering south to the Atlantic coastal states and the Gulf of Mexico. In the north and east of its range it is the most abundant dabbling duck, replacing the Mallard *A. platyrhynchos,* which is largely absent from that part, and occupying the same habitat. Despite its presence in eastern North America very few birds have wandered across the Atlantic, with records from the Azores, Ireland (4), England (7), and Sweden.

The species has the same size and build as Mallard and in overall appearance resembles very dark female Mallard. Unfortunately hybrids with Mallard occur readily and are intermediate in character, while dark-plumaged Mallard containing some domestic blood add further to identification problems. The adult male (1) is sooty brown above and below, with a noticeably paler head and neck, showing more contrast than a female Mallard. The bill is yellow compared with the Mallard's dull orange-brown. The adult female (2) is not quite so dark as the male, with more grey on the head and neck, and less well-defined patterning on the body feathers. The bill is olive-green and black. The immature (3) is even more like a Mallard though the bill still shows olive-green.

All plumages of the Black Duck lack any of the white or very pale areas showing in the tail of the Mallard, and the speculum has a single thin white bar at the rear not the broader front and rear stripes of the Mallard.

The Black Duck's voice is almost identical to the Mallard's.

20 Pintail *Anas acuta*

The Pintail breeds around pools and marshes across much of northern Eurasia and North America, though numbers in Europe away from Scandinavia and USSR are small. It winters on estuaries and some inland floods in western Europe (c. 50 000 birds), Mediterranean–Black Sea area (250 000), and in tropical Africa, India, Far East, and North and Central America.

The male (1) is slender with greatly elongated central tail feathers. The combination of chocolate head and long neck, contrasting with the white stripe running down the side of the neck to meet the pale grey upperparts and white underparts renders it unmistakable. The black undertail coverts are set off by a creamy band in front. The long tail feathers and drooping scaulars are black, edged white. The bill and feet are blue-grey.

The female (2) is also slender and long-necked, with a pointed not elongated tail. Her overall colour is paler than other dabbling ducks and the pale buff crescentic flank markings are prominent. The underparts are whitish and unmarked, the bill and feet grey.

The eclipse male (3) is greyer than the adult female, especially in the head and neck, and also lacks the buff flank marks.

The downy young (6) has a distinctive white stripe above and below the dark eyestripe. The juveniles are difficult to distinguish from the adult female but the male (4) has more brightly coloured wings than the female (5). Both are rather darker above than the adult female, lacking her pale feather edgings, and are more streaked and spotted on the chest and belly.

21 Garganey *Anas querquedula*

This is Europe's only summer visiting duck. It breeds on shallow fresh waters and marshes throughout northern Eurasia, though is patchily distributed in north-west Europe where it has recently declined. Small numbers winter in the Mediterranean basin, but it is most numerous in tropical Africa, with perhaps 250 000 in West Africa alone. It also winters in India and south and east Asia.

The Garganey is similar in size to the Teal *A. crecca,* though can appear slimmer, with its slightly longer neck and bill. The most prominent feature of the adult male (1) is the white head stripe running well down the nape and contrasting with the dark red-brown head. The sharp division between the brown breast and the pale grey flanks and white belly is also very conspicuous. The bold eyestripe alone should prevent confusion with any other species, as should the dry rattling call.

The adult female (2) is very similar to other female dabbling ducks, especially the Teal, though paler and the throat whiter. The pale patch at the base of the long bill, and the more distinct dark eyestripe are useful closer-range identification features.

The eclipse male (3) closely resembles the adult female, though is not quite so pale and has whiter underparts. In flight the pale blue forewing is much brighter than the female's.

Two complete dark stripes on the head help to distinguish the downy young (5) from that of the Teal. Juvenile Garganey (4) are also like the adult female, but show more mottling on the underparts. The males show few signs of adult plumage before they leave Europe in the autumn.

22 Blue-winged Teal *Anas discors*

The Blue-winged Teal is a North American duck breeding right across the continent but mainly in the prairies beside small pools and ditches. In winter it is found in marshes and coastal lagoons in the southern states, Mexico and south to northern South America. The status in the West Palearctic is confused by escapes from captivity but some wild birds do occur as recoveries of Canadian ringed birds have been made in England, Spain, and Morocco. There are over 70 sightings in England and Ireland, and scattered reports from other west European countries.

The adult male (1) has a very distinctive head pattern. The bright pale blue of the forewing will show if the wing is drooped even slightly. The adult female (2) is much like a female Teal *A. crecca* when at rest and if none of the blue forewing is showing. The Teal is rather paler, with a smaller bill, and lacks the white spot at the base of the bill. Confusion is possible with escaped Cinnamon Teal *A. cyanoptera*, which have longer, broader bills, and less contrast between light and dark areas on the head. The body plumage is typically warmer and richer in tone.

The immature Bluewing (3) is similarly close in appearance to a Teal and separable on the same features as the adult female.

Bluewings make little noise, the male having a soft 'peep' the female a high-pitched quack.

23 Shoveler *Anas clypeata*

The Shoveler breeds throughout northern Eurasia, (though locally in western Europe) and in the western half of the northern North America. The main breeding habitat is small pools in open woodland, grassland, and steppe. A few birds are resident but the majority move south to winter in shallow fresh waters reaching central America, West and East Africa, India, and south-east Asia. The total population of the west Palearctic has been put at one and a half million.

The Shoveler has a very distinctive silhouette, sitting low in the water, the flattened head ending in the huge spatulate bill. The brilliant white chest of the male (1) contrasts with the dark head and chestnut flanks to render it unmistakable. Although an adult female's colour (2) is closest to that of a Mallard *A. platyrhynchos*, the size of the head and bill and the squat shape should leave no room for confusion.

Eclipse male Shoveler (3) resemble adult females as in other dabbling ducks, but the upper parts are darker and less spotted. Shovelers are slow to emerge from eclipse, moulting some body feathers twice, first into a supplementary plumage (4) and finally back into breeding dress by December. The immature (5) has more uniform upperparts and more streaked underparts than the adult female. The downy young (6) is darker above than the Mallard and the bill quickly becomes rather broad.

Male Shovelers make a distinctive 'tuk tuk' call, mainly in flight; the female has a low quack.

Adult breeding plumage

The male Mandarin (**1**) in flight shows a large head and a blue speculum with a white trailing edge. The orange 'sails' show as patches on the wings rather than standing up as shown. The female (**2**) has a pale belly and a white trailing edge.

Marbled Teal (**3**) look to have no speculum in flight and this evenly coloured wing is very distinctive. The crest makes the head appear large.

The male Falcated Duck (**4**) is another bird showing a large head. Its pale forewing and green and black speculum edged with white are distinctive. The female (**5**) is like a stubby female Mallard but with a prominent pale forewing and dark, white-edged speculum.

Both sexes of the Mallard in flight show a broad purple-blue speculum bordered with black and white fore and aft. The dark head and black tail of the male (**6**) stand out. The belly of the female (**7**) is brown unlike most other dabbling ducks.

Male (**8**) and female (**9**) Black Duck look very dark in flight with no white on the tail or at the front of the speculum, thus distinguishing them from Mallard.

Male Gadwall (**10**) have a unique white speculum with black and chestnut also on the wings. The black rump is conspicuous. The female (**11**) shows some white on the speculum and has a white belly unlike the Mallard.

The long neck and elongated tail feathers of the male Pintail (**12**) give it an unmistakable silhouette quite apart from the white neck and coloured speculum. The female (**13**) is also slender with a conspicuous white trailing edge to the wings.

The male Wigeon (**14**) has a very conspicuous white forewing showing at a considerable distance, when it also appears to be a light bird with a dark head. The short-necked appearance of the female (**15**) and her green, white-bordered speculum, are good identification features.

The male American Wigeon (**16**) is similar to the male Wigeon but overall is a darker bird with a light head. The female (**17**) is lighter underneath than the Wigeon with white not grey axilliaries.

Apart from their small size male Teal (**18**) show two prominent white stripes down the back and two pale lines either side of the speculum. The female (**19**) has well-defined white bars on the wing.

The broad white border to the speculum of the Cape Teal (**20**) combined with uniform pale plumage are its most distinguishing features.

The grey-blue forewing identifies the male Garganey (**21**) coupled with the very conspicuous white head stripe and sharp border between chest and belly. The female (**22**) has a pale grey forewing and indistinct speculum. Both sexes show a dark leading edge when viewed from underneath.

The Blue-winged Teal male (**23**) has a much bluer forewing than the Garganey and no white trailing edge to the wing. The head stripe is less visible. The female (**24**) has a bluer forewing than the Garganey, little white on the wing and a dark speculum.

The heavy-headed look of the Shoveler is enhanced by the wings seeming to be set well back. The white chest and scapulars of the male (**25**) are very conspicuous. The grey-blue forewing and green speculum help to identify the female(**26**).

25 Red-crested Pochard *Netta rufina*

The Red-crested Pochard breeds locally in well-vegetated pools and slow-flowing rivers in many European countries north to Denmark, and also by larger waters in southern USSR. The more northerly birds migrate to the Mediterranean, Pakistan, India, and Burma. It has been increasing and spreading in recent years in north-west Europe moving on to smaller waters such as gravel pits. There are probably about 20 000 in north-west Europe and 50 000 in the Mediterranean–Black Sea area. Many hundreds of thousands live in the USSR.

The large rounded head of the male (1) with its golden chestnut colour, and the bright red bill, make it unmistakable. The black chest and white sides are also very distinctive. The female (2) often looks quite long-necked when sitting on the water, while her pale cheeks and dark brown cap coming down to the eye are excellent identification features. She usually has a little pink or red on the sides of the bill.

The eclipse male (3) retains the bright red bill of the breeding plumage but otherwise becomes much like the female, though the head is larger-looking and the body darker. The juvenile (4) is also similar to the female but duller and more grey. Recognizable adult plumage begins to be acquired from about September. The downy young (5) is rather pale for a diving duck and has a fairly complete eyestripe.

Neither sex calls much except during the breeding season when the male has a hoarse wheeze and a far-carrying croak, while the female uses a low guttural churr.

26 Pochard *Aythya ferina*

The breeding range of the Pochard extends from western Europe (where it is rather local, though increasing and spreading) through the grassland and steppe regions of western and central USSR as far as Lake Baikal. It avoids forested and tundra areas. Some birds are resident but the majority move west and south to winter on fresh waters in western Europe, the Mediterranean, East Africa, Iran, India, south-east Asia, and Japan. About 250 000 winter in north-west Europe and perhaps three times that number in the Mediterranean–Black Sea region.

Pochard have a hump-backed short-necked silhouette on the water enhanced by the tail remaining mostly flat along the water. The combination of chestnut head, black breast and tail, and very pale grey back and flanks of the male (1) are unique among European diving ducks. The adult female (2) has distinctive pale feathering on the face and a combination of brown head and chest and greyish body. The high crown and long sloping forehead help to distinguish her from other female diving ducks.

In eclipse the male (3) has a uniform golden-brown head and neck and grey back, but is otherwise like the female. So also is the immature (4) though with much less grey and more barring on the chest and belly. Adult plumage is assumed from October onwards. The downy young (5) are fairly dark above but with pale cheeks, an indistinct eyestripe, and a dull cheek spot.

Male Pochard are almost entirely silent except for a soft whistle during courtship. The male has the typical diving duck churr.

27 Ring-necked Duck *Aythya collaris*

This species breeds in pools in forested lowlands right across North America, wintering in swamps and marshes around the Gulf of Mexico and on the Pacific Coast. In the last fifty years it has greatly extended its range to the east of the Great Lakes. Linked with this expansion there have been increasing occurrences in Europe. Britain and Ireland have had nearly 100 sightings, with fewer in most other west European countries.

The adult male Ringneck (**1**) is superficially like a male Tufted Duck *A. fuligula*. The most obvious difference is the head shape, rounded in the Tufted Duck but flat-topped and coming to a peak at the rear of the crown in the Ringneck. Another prominent feature is the pure white at the front of the flanks running up to form a spur in front of the closed wing. Close to, the white stripes over the base and near the tip of the bill are diagnostic.

Adult females (**2**) show only a small amount of whitish at the base of the bill (cf. the more extensive white on female Tufted Duck and Scaup *A. marila*) and a distinct white 'spectacle' round the eye. The head is more pointed than the Tufted Duck's and there is a white band behind the bill tip. Juvenile Ringnecks (**3**) closely resemble the female, including head shape, but are darker above with less obvious head and bill markings.

Calls of Ringnecks are soft and like other diving ducks.

28 Ferruginous Duck *Aythya nyroca*

The Ferruginous Duck is restricted to lowland temperate wetlands largely in western and southern USSR, but extending into Kashmir and southern Tibet. It is a local breeder in most eastern European countries with outliers in France and Spain. Mainly migratory it winters on large fresh or coastal waters round the Mediterranean, south of the Sahara, and in Pakistan and India. Decreases have been noted in many parts of the range this century. The population wintering in the Mediterranean–Black Sea area has been estimated at 75 000 birds.

The adult male Ferruginous Duck (**1**) is readily identifiable from its all-over reddish-chestnut plumage and conspicuous white undertail, which is visible at considerable distances. The white eye shows up well at closer range. Adult females (**2**) are duller and browner than the males and can be distinguished from female Tufted Ducks *A. fuligula* by the white undertail coverts which a few Tufted Ducks possess but never as extensive or well-defined. Ferruginous Ducks are also more slender and have a higher crown.

The eclipse male (**3**) is much like an adult female but more red-brown in tone on the head and breast. The white eye and white undertail coverts are retained. The immature (**4**) is more uniform above than the adult female and the white undertail is partially obscured by brown markings. The downy young (**5**) is very dark above and golden-yellow below with almost no face markings.

Male Ferruginous Ducks have a range of soft calls; the female makes the usual harsh growl of female diving ducks.

29 Tufted Duck *Aythya fuligula*

The Tufted Duck breeds on small lowland fresh waters in Iceland, most of Britain and Ireland, locally elsewhere in western Europe, and from Scandinavia across the northern part of USSR to the Pacific. Winter quarters are on fresh and brackish waters in north-west Europe, the Mediterranean, East Africa, Iran, India, south-east Asia, China, and Japan. There has been a marked increase and spread in the west of the range this century. There are an estimated 525 000 birds in north-west Europe in winter and a further 300 000 in the Mediterranean–Black Sea region.

The black and white adult male (**1**) with its small hanging crest is unmistakable (though see Ring-necked Duck *A. collaris*). The adult female in summer (**2**) also has a small crest and is shorter and dumpier than a female Scaup *A. marila*. In winter the female becomes whiter on the flanks and may have a little white on the face (**3**) or a considerable amount (**4**) when the similarity with Scaup grows, though size and head shape are still diagnostic.

The adult male in eclipse (**5**) has darker upperparts and paler flanks than the female and never any white on the face. The immature male (**6**) reaches this near-adult stage by December though with grey-brown tinging to the flanks and undertail and a very short crest. The female at this age (**7**) is very like the adult though lacking a crest or more than a trace of white on the face. The downy young (**8**) is sooty brown above, lighter below, with indistinct facial markings.

The male whistles softly during courtship; the female has a low churr.

30 Scaup *Aythya marila*

The Scaup nests by tundra and forest pools in northern Eurasia and North America, wintering mainly on shallow seas of sheltered coasts to the south. In Europe there are breeding populations in Iceland, northern Scandinavia, and round the Gulf of Bothnia. Wintering flocks are found particularly in the Baltic and on North Sea coasts with an estimated total of 150 000 birds. There are a further 50 000 in the Mediterranean–Black Sea area.

The adult male Scaup (**1**) is the only diving duck to show a combination of dark head and chest, white sides, and pale grey back. The adult female in summer (**2**) can be told from female Tufted Ducks by her broader body and larger head and by the white on the face including a patch behind the eye which the Tufted Duck never has. This patch is lost in the winter, however, (**4**) and more attention must be paid to size and shape, though few Tufted Duck show as large or as clearly defined a white area round the base of the bill.

The eclipse male is more like an adult male than most other ducks and much less like the female. The immature male (**5**) has grey flecking on the back absent in the female (**6**) and both show a capped appearance from the pale cheeks, though with little white round the bill. The downy young (**7**) has a more pronounced face pattern than the Tufted Duck and is not quite so dark.

Scaup make little noise outside the courtship period when the male utters a soft 'coo' and the female the usual low 'kurr'.

N.W.CUSA.

31 Eider *Somateria mollissima*

Eider Ducks breed on virtually all arctic coasts except central arctic USSR, and in northern Britain, the Baltic, the Sea of Okhotsk, and Nova Scotia. The range has extended southwards in western Europe this century. There is some southward movement in winter. The population of north-west Europe has been estimated at two million birds, principally in the Baltic and round the Norwegian coasts.

The adult male Eider Duck (1) is completely distinctive, no other bird having the same pattern of black and white. Differentiation of females and immatures from other eiders (q.v.) is often difficult, sometimes impossible unless at very close range. The head shape, feathering round the bill, and the pattern of barring are often critical. Breeding adult females (2) are a warm brown, less rusty-toned than the female King Eider *S. spectabilis*. In autumn (6) they become darker and lose some of the buff edgings to the body feathers. Males in eclipse (3) are mainly sooty-brown, flecked white on the head and chest, and retaining the white wing-coverts.

Immature males go through a series of moults to reach adult plumage and present a curious piebald appearance. Many look very dark except for a white chest, gradually becoming white on the back (5). In the second year (4) the male becomes much more like the adult though with brown feathers showing in the white areas. The downy young (7) is dark grey above, paler beneath, with few markings.

Male Eiders have a double or treble-noted cooing call; females make a low growling sound.

32 King Eider *Somateria spectabilis*

This species breeds entirely north of the Arctic Circle in the West Palearctic, in Spitsbergen, and USSR, coming south of it only in winter, along the Norwegian coast and in Iceland. It breeds right along the arctic coast of USSR, and round the coasts of arctic Canada and Greenland. The population of the west Palearctic is unknown but it is estimated that there may be one to one and a half million adults in the whole of the USSR.

The adult male King Eider (1) is unmistakable in both plumage and silhouette, especially the large head and two small black 'sails'. The adult female (2) is quite like the female Eider *S. mollissima* though more rusty-brown in colour, while at close range the smaller bare shield above the bill, the pale chin, and the thin dark line separating the slightly shaggy nape from the cheeks are useful features. The eclipse male (3) is noticeably dark except for paler areas on the cheeks, throat, and chest. The wing coverts remain white. The frontal shield shrinks, losing some of the unique head-shape.

Juvenile King Eiders (5) are very like females but lack the rusty tone of the plumage so that separation from young Eiders has to rely on the feathering round the bill. Second-year males (4) are close to adults having been through similar piebald stages to the Eider. The downy young (6) are paler than the Eider with a distinct eyestripe.

The cooing call of the male King Eider is coarser and more tremulous than the Eider's. The female's croak is deeper and hoarser.

N.W.CUSA.

33 Spectacled Eider *Somateria fischeri*

The Spectacled Eider only occurs as a vagrant to Europe, off the arctic coasts of north-western USSR, and the arctic and Atlantic coasts of Norway. It breeds along the coast of north-east Siberia, on St. Lawrence Island, and in northern and western Alaska. It withdraws from the breeding range for the winter, moving to open water in the Bering Sea south of the ice-edge, particularly on the Siberian side.

The remarkable head-shape and pattern of the adult male (1) allows of no confusion with any other species. Even at great distances the presence of a black chest and absence of black on the head will exclude Eider *S. mollissima*. The adult female (2) is greyer on the head, rather yellow in tone and on the body and lacks such prominent barring as other eiders. However, the similarity to the female Eider is strong and only the pale patch round the eye and the feathering coming well down the upper mandible are sure identification guides. The duller plumage tone and long sloping forehead are further distinctions from the female King Eider *S. spectabilis*.

The eclipse male (3) is rather dark grey-brown, though paler than other eclipse male Eiders. The heavy-headed look and eye-patches are still noticeable.

Spectacled Eiders call much less than Eiders or King Eiders. The male has a weak double cooing-call; the female a croaking sound.

34 Steller's Eider *Polysticta stelleri*

The principal breeding range of this species is confined to the arctic coasts of north-east Siberia and Alaska. The wintering range lies to the south in the southern Bering Sea. However, small flocks summer and irregular breeding takes place well outside these areas including in central and western Siberia, Novaya Zemlya, and northern Norway. In the last area up to 400 birds have been seen in recent years, and breeding has occured. Stragglers are seen south to the Baltic and adjacent North Sea, and in Scotland.

Steller's Eider is a small duck, much smaller than Eider *Somateria mollissima,* shaped not unlike a dabbling duck *Anas* with its small rounded head, rather straight back, and pointed tail carried clear of the water. The adult male (1) has a unique plumage pattern, with no black along the waterline except at the tail (cf. other eiders). The adult female (2) is rather uniformly dark, and more mottled than barred compared with other eiders. The blue and white speculum, which shows when the wing is opened, and drooping scapulars are important characteristics.

In eclipse (3), the male Steller's Eider becomes like the female overall, but retains a hint of the head and chest pattern from the breeding plumage, and the upper wing-coverts stay white above the blue speculum.

The juvenile (4) is paler than the adult female, especially underneath, with paler tips to the feathers of the back, and the chest and underparts are strongly barred. The downy young (5) is sepia above, paler below.

Calls of both sexes are restricted to low growls and guttural notes.

35 Harlequin *Histrionicus histrionicus*

The only breeding area for this species in Europe is in Iceland where there is a resident population of up to 3000 pairs, living in fast-flowing rivers and streams, wintering mainly on the coast. Elsewhere Harlequins breed in west Greenland, eastern Canada, western USA and Alaska, and eastern USSR. Vagrants have been reported from several European countries.

The adult male Harlequin (**1**) is most aptly named for its patterned plumage, quite unlike any other duck. At extreme range it can look very dark, when its small size, cocked-up tail, and buoyancy will still be noticeable. No other small duck has the same pattern of white on the face as the adult female Harlequin (**2**). The much larger Scoters *Melanitta* have only two white spots and no white round the bill. The eclipse male (**3**) is very like the female but blacker, tinged grey-blue on the back, and the white face patches are more distinct. Some white is retained on the inner wing feathers and this may show along the back.

Juvenile Harlequins (**5**) are very like adult females, if paler. Males begin to acquire adult plumage from about October, and by the spring are beginning to look a little bit like a mixture of male and female (**4**). Downy young Harlequins (**6**) have a distinct dark crown to below the eye, and very white cheeks and underparts.

Harlequins are not very vocal birds. The male has a low piping whistle; the female gives a harsh croak.

36 Long-tailed Duck *Clangula hyemalis*

Long-tailed Ducks have a circumpolar distribution breeding in tundra and scrub uplands in the arctic and near-arctic of Eurasia, North America, and Greenland. They winter on ice-free arctic coasts, and south to north-west Europe, north-west United States and the northern Pacific. True numbers are difficult to estimate but up to five million have been suggested for the western USSR. The north-west European wintering population may lie between a half and one million.

Four separate plumages have been recognized in adult male and adult female Longtails. Only the more important and long-lasting ones are shown here. The adult male in breeding (**1**), eclipse (**2**), and wintering (**3**) plumage is unmistakable, with his slender shape and greatly elongated tail feathers. The white-headed, white-bodied winter plumage (**3**) lasts from about October to April. At other times the chest, back, and wings become brown.

The adult female's breeding plumage is not shown but is similar to her autumn (**5**) and winter (**4**) plumage except that there is more black on the head, mantle, and rump. The white body and extent of white on the head distinguish the female Longtail from all other ducks.

Juvenile Longtails (**7**) have a dark-capped, white-cheeked appearance. Males in their first autumn (**6**) acquire more white on the head and flanks, and the tail begins to grow. The downy young (**8**) has pale spots in front of and above the eye.

The male Longtail has a melodious, yodelling three- or four-note call; the female has a low soft quack.

37 Common Scoter *Melanitta nigra*

The Common Scoter breeds locally in Iceland, Ireland and Scotland, and from northern Scandinavia across northern USSR to the Pacific and Alaska. The easternmost birds, together with those in Alaska and a scattering in Canada belong to the race *americana*. Breeding takes place by large lakes, marshes, and slow-moving rivers. Wintering is exclusively in shallow areas of sheltered coastal waters, from northern Norway to the west coast of North Africa, on the Atlantic seaboard of North America, and on both sides of the northern Pacific. The winter population of the West Palearctic has been variously estimated to lie between a half and one and a half million.

The adult male (1) is the only all-black waterfowl with no white anywhere. The squat shape, heavy bill, and rather long tail are characteristic.

The adult female (2) has conspicuous white cheeks (cf. the white face spots of female Velvet *M. fusca* and Surf Scoter *M. perspicillata*) and a distinct capped appearance. The eclipse plumage is very slightly duller than the breeding dress and browner underneath.

The juvenile Common Scoter (5) is very like the adult female but paler brown above and whiter below. From December the immature male (4) develops some black mottling on the head, upperparts and flanks, gradually becoming blackheaded, while orange begins to appear on the bill. The downy young (5) has dark upperparts and breast but a whitish chin and throat.

During courtship the male utters a low musical piping of several notes. The female makes a number of hoarse grating calls.

38 Surf Scoter *Melanitta perspicillata*

This species does not breed in Europe but occurs almost annually as a vagrant. There have been over 100 records in Britain and Ireland, particularly in Shetland and Orkney, and several in Scandinavia and France, with fewer reports from several other European countries. The breeding range is from western Alaska through central Canada to Labrador. Breeding takes place by lakes and pools in open boreal regions. In winter it is found on the Pacific and Atlantic coasts of North America.

Adult male Surf Scoters (1) are readily identified at close range by the curiously multicoloured bill and the white forehead and nape. The white patches should be visible at considerable distances. The tail is markedly longer than the Common Scoter's *M. nigra*. The adult female (2) closely resembles the female Velvet Scoter *M. fusca* being distinguishable at rest only by the rather faint pale nape patch and the heavier bill. The clinching feature is the white on the wing of the Velvet Scoter, which fortunately often shows even when the bird is at rest.

Juveniles (4) are much paler than the adult female with almost white breast and belly. The head spots are less clear-cut and often run together when compared with those on the young Velvet Scoter. Again the latter have white in the wing. Immature males (3) get a white nape patch though none on the forehead and some colour in the bill by the spring.

Surf Scoters are virtually silent outside the breeding season.

39 Velvet Scoter *Melanitta fusca*

Velvet Scoters breed around the coasts of the eastern Baltic and the Gulf of Bothnia, and in the boreal and montane regions of northern Scandinavia and the USSR, with an isolated population in eastern Turkey. Elsewhere they breed through the forested areas of the USSR to the Pacific coast, and in Alaska and the western half of Canada. The easternmost USSR birds and those in North America form a separate race *deglandi*. Velvet Scoters winter mainly on coasts in north-west Europe, the Black Sea, the Atlantic coast of North America and both sides of the northern Pacific. The West Palearctic population in winter has been put at about 200 000.

The adult male (**1**) looks all black at a distance and so like the male Common Scoter *M. nigra* unless the wings are flapped exposing the large white panel on the secondaries. Closer to, the yellow sides not top, to the bill, and the white eye mark, can be seen. The adult female (**2**) is differentiated from the female Surf Scoter *M. perspicillata* (q.v.) by the white in the wing and the lack of a pale nape patch.

Juvenile Velvet Scoters (**5**) closely resemble adult females though paler and browner and with whiter face patches. Young males darken through the winter, becoming nearly black by the spring (**4**), and developing some yellow on the bill. The downy young (**6**) are very like those of Common Scoter but whiter on the chin and underneath.

Velvet Scoters rarely call.

40 Bufflehead *Bucephala albeola*

The Bufflehead is a native of the wooded lowlands of North America where it breeds in holes in trees and earth banks beside lakes, pools, and slow-moving rivers. The range extends from central Alaska into western Canada, then across central Canada to Ontario. Small numbers breed in northern Oregon and California. Wintering takes place principally in shallow sheltered seas on the coasts of the Pacific south as far as Mexico, the Gulf of Mexico, and the Atlantic, and on some larger inland waters. There have been a handful of European records: five in England, and one each in Iceland and Czechoslovakia.

The Bufflehead is about the size of a Teal *Anas crecca* but more compact and lower in the water. The head is noticeably large. The adult male is quite distinct with its black and white body and large wedge-shaped white patch on the back of the head. The adult female (**2**) is only likely to be confused with female Harlequin *Histrionicus histrionicus* and Longtail *B. clangula*, but both are rather larger and have more than the single bold white patch on the face. In eclipse (**3**) the male looks much like the female though with a blacker head and a larger white face patch. In non-breeding plumage (**5**), the female becomes browner and paler.

Immature males (**4**) are like a dark female with a larger face patch and so close in appearance to the eclipse male.

Buffleheads are generally silent apart from a repeated guttural call sometimes given by the male.

41 Barrow's Goldeneye *Bucephala islandica*

Within Europe the Barrow's Goldeneye only breeds in Iceland. It is resident there, and confined to Lake Myvatn (about 800 breeding pairs) and other waters in the north-west. The birds are virtually non-migratory staying through the winter on ice-free areas of the lakes. Vagrants have occurred in several west-European countries. Elsewhere the Barrow's Goldeneye occurs on the west side of North America, from California to Alaska, with isolated populations in Labrador and West Greenland.

The Barrow's Goldeneye has always to be distinguished from the Goldeneye *B. clangula* (q.v.), even in Iceland where the latter winters in very small numbers. The adult male (1) is a stumpy, large-headed, black and white duck with a large white crescent on its face, and a row of white blobs on its scapulars. The adult female (2) can be separated from all ducks other than the Goldeneye by her dark brown head, white neck, and grey-brown body. The female Goldeneye has more white on the wings and scapulars, but separation is difficult. The eclipse male (3) closely resembles her but has a greyer head and all black bill.

The juvenile (5) resembles the adult female too, but the head is duller, the body browner, and the white collar virtually absent. The face crescent appears on the immature male (4) as early as November. The downy young has a grey bill, not black as in the Goldeneye.

Barrow's Goldeneye are not very vocal birds, the male grunting during courtship, the female uttering a high-pitched croak.

42 Goldeneye *Bucephala clangula*

The Goldeneye breeds near pools and rivers in coniferous forests, across northern Eurasia and across northern North America, except the extreme west. Small numbers breed on the edges of the range in Scotland, West and East Germany, Czechoslovakia, and Poland. Goldeneye migrate south for the winter to north-west and central Europe, the eastern Mediterranean, Black and Caspian Seas, both sides of the Pacific, and central and southern North America. The European wintering population has been estimated at 200 000, with a further 20 000 in the Mediterranean–Black Sea area.

The adult male (1) shows much more white on the sides than the Barrow's Goldeneye *B. islandica* (q.v.) and has only a round white spot on the face, compared with the latter's large white crescent. The adult female (2) is very similar to the Barrow's Goldeneye female but has a duller brown head and less yellow on the tip of a finer bill. The eclipse male (3) resembles the adult female though with a darker head and more white on the scapulars. This latter feature distinguishes it from the Barrow's Goldeneye.

Juveniles (5) lack the white collar of the adult female and are doubtfully distinguishable from juvenile Barrow's Goldeneye. The immature male (4) develops a darker head and the white face spot by November, when white begins to appear on the scapulars. The downy young (6) differs from the Barrow's Goldeneye only in its black not grey bill.

Both sexes are silent except during courtship. In flight the wings make a very distinctive whistling sound, identifiably different from the wing sound of Barrow's Goldeneye.

43 Hooded Merganser *Mergus cucullatus*

This species is a rare vagrant to Europe. There are just three records from Ireland, one from Wales, and one from West Germany. It breeds in wooded areas of North America, discontinuously from south-east Alaska to Nova Scotia, though principally in southern Canada and north-east USA. It winters on both sides of the continent, on fresh and brackish waters.

The Hooded Merganser is a rather small, short-bodied duck with an elongated crested head and fine bill. The adult male (1) is immediately identified by his remarkable fan-shaped crest of white bordered with black. This is not erect all the time and when lying flat shows as black with a central white bar. The black and white bars in front of the chestnut flanks, and the black and white drooping scapulars are also very distinctive. The adult female (2) is superficially like a female Red-breasted Merganser *M. serrator* (q.v.) but smaller and with a shorter bill. The latter is also paler and greyer on the back and has a much less pronounced crest. When closed the female Hooded Merganser's crest shows as a prominent backward extension to the head. The eclipse male (not illustrated) closely resembles the adult female but has a black bill and retains at least some white on the head.

Juveniles resemble the adult female though with a much shorter crest. The young males (3) acquire some white on the crest, breast bars, and scapulars by early winter.

44 Smew *Mergus albellus*

The Smew breeds in coniferous and mixed forests from northern Scandinavia to eastern Siberia. It also breeds further south as far as the Volga delta. The winter quarters are on fresh water or sheltered sea inlets scattered through north-west, central, and south-east Europe, around the Caspian and Aral Seas, as well as in China and Japan. About 20 000 winter in north-west and central Europe, and perhaps 50 000 in south-east Europe and the Black and Caspian Seas.

The Smew is only slightly larger than the Teal *Anas crecca*. The adult male (10) is unique among ducks for the amount of white showing, with only small patches or fine lines of black. The adult female (2 and 4) has a diagnostic white face and dark rufous crown and nape. For the rest her body is mainly grey and greyish white. The eclipse male (3) is darker on the back than the female and slightly redder on the head. It lacks the black face patch but retains a larger area of white on the wing-coverts.

The juvenile Smew (5) is very similar to the adult female, though browner on the back and lacking the black face patch, or virtually any white on the wings. The immatures gain some indication of adult plumage by the early winter. The downy young is like a smaller version of the Goldeneye *B. clangula* but with a narrower bill.

Smew very rarely call except during display or when alarmed. The male makes a soft rattling noise, while the female has a hoarse 'krrr'.

45 Red-breasted Merganser *Mergus serrator*

The Red-breasted Merganser breeds from temperate coasts and rivers through the forested zone to the arctic tundra, as has a complete circumpolar distribution. Most birds are at least partially migratory wintering mainly on coasts. North-west Europe and the Mediterranean and Black Seas are major wintering areas as are China and Japan, all coasts of North America, and those of Iceland and West Greenland. About 40 000 are thought to winter in north-west Europe and 50 000 in the Mediterranean–Black Sea region.

The adult male Red-breasted Merganser (1) is quite unmistakable with its elongated shape, crest, and long, thin bill. The combination of dark crested head, white neck and dark chest should prevent any confusion with male Goosander *M. merganser,* which is additionally white on the flanks and lacks a crest. The adult female (2) can also be distinguished from the Goosander by its ragged crest and by the more mottled back and dark flanks, and lack of a sharp demarcation between the neck and chest. Red-breasted Mergansers are at least 10 per cent smaller than Goosanders but this is not always apparent. In eclipse the male (3) resembles the adult female but has a darker back and more white on the wings.

The immature female (4) can only be distinguished from the adult by her shorter crest and the presence of more white on the chest and lower flanks. The downy young (5) has two poorly defined black lines on its face which is suffused with tawny.

The male has various display calls, the female makes a harsh 'krrr'.

46 Goosander *Mergus merganser*

Although the range of the Goosander overlaps that of the Red-breasted Merganser *M. serrator,* having a circumpolar distribution in the forested zone, it favours inland waters and upper reaches of rivers and avoids the coast. Wintering takes place largely on fresh waters or on very sheltered coasts in north-west Europe, the Black and Caspian Seas, northern India, China and Japan, and across central North America. The north-west European winter population is thought to number about 75 000 birds with a further 10 000 in the Mediterranean–Black Sea area.

The adult male Goosander (1) has a rather bulbous head and long bill, the dark green head and back and white chest and flanks distinctly different from the smaller and crested Red-breasted Merganser (q.v.). Adult female Goosanders (2) are red-brown on the head with a grey or grey-white body. The head has an obvious crest but thicker and tidier than the Red-breasted Merganser's. There is a clear white patch under the chin. The eclipse male (3) is much darker than the female on the upperparts and a considerable amount of white shows on the sides.

The juvenile Goosander (4) is essentially like the adult female but has a distinct pale stripe between the base of the bill and the eye. The crest is quite short and it and the head are more buff-brown than reddish. The bill is yellow-brown not red. The downy young (5) has well-defined stripes on the head and tawny only on the nape.

Neither sex calls much except during display.

47 Ruddy Duck   *Oxyura jamaicensis*

The North American race of the Ruddy Duck *O. j. jamaicensis* breeds in north and west central North America wintering south to California, Mexico, and Florida. It is also resident in the West Indies. Three other races breed in South America. Ruddy Ducks have bred in southern Britain since 1960 following escapes from captivity. They have spread and increased to a current 1500 birds. There are movements within the country during the winter but none away.

Ruddy Ducks are small, dumpy, very short-necked ducks with a long stiff tail which may be held up or laid on the water. The body colour of the adult male (**1**) is truly ruddy. The black cap, white face, and bright blue bill add further to its unique appearance. The adult female (**3**) has a dark brown cap and nape and an indistinct cheek stripe. Otherwise she is brown, reddish above, very pale below. The male's eclipse plumage (**2**) is assumed in late July and kept right through the winter until March. Superficially like the adult female, the main points of difference are the pure white cheeks and undertail coverts, darker cap, and the presence of some chestnut on the back.

The juvenile (**4**) is much like the adult female but greyer and duller on the head and back, and more barred on the back. The downy young (**5**) is very sooty-brown with a narrow dark streak on the white cheek and some pale grey on the breast.

Ruddy Ducks utter few calls though both sexes make rattling noises when beating their bills against their chests during display.

48 White-headed Duck   *Oxyura leucocephala*

The White-headed Duck has a fragmented distribution in southern Spain, North Africa, Bulgaria, Turkey, and southern USSR, particularly to the east and north of the Aral Sea. It breeds on shallow chiefly fresh waters and winters in similar habitat generally not far from the breeding range but also south to Egypt, south Caspian, Iraq, Iran, and northern India. It is a vagrant north to several European countries. The population in the western Mediterranean is estimated at 2000 birds.

The adult male (**1**) has a large rounded head with a blue bill swollen at the base, giving it a very distinctive silhouette. The body is grey and red-brown above and grey-brown underneath. The tail is held either cocked up or flat in the water. The adult female (**2**) is rather like the female Ruddy Duck *O. jamaicensis* but larger, has a swollen base to the bill and a better defined stripe across a paler cheek. The eclipse male (**3**) also resembles the Ruddy Duck but apart from the head and bill shape has more white on the head, including a white forehead. This plumage is kept from August to April.

The juvenile White-headed Duck (**4**) is female-like though duller and paler, and separated from Ruddy Duck on the paleness of the cheek and obvious stripe across it. The downy young (**5**) has greyer cheeks than the Ruddy Duck and lacks pale grey on the breast.

White-headed Ducks are silent except for a few grunts, piping calls and wheezes made during display.

1. Adult breeding plumage

Red-crested Pochard males (**1**) show a unique white leading edge as well as a broad white wing bar behind. The white underparts are also conspicuous. The large rounded head dominates the flight silhouette. The female (**2**) similarly has a broad white wing bar.

Male Pochard (**3**) have a pale grey wing bar contrasting with the darker forewing. The dark head, neck, and chest; light body; and dark tail form a useful identification pattern. The female's wing pattern (**4**) is the same as the male's and so different from other female diving ducks.

In flight the male Ring-necked Duck (**5**) reveals pale grey wing bars on a black and white duck — a unique combination. The female (**6**) has less grey on the wing than the female Pochard and is pale underneath.

The Ferruginous Duck male (**7**) looks reddish in flight with a white wing bar running almost to the tip. The female (**8**) has the same wing bar and a whitish belly. The Tufted Duck female has a shorter wing bar and a brownish belly.

The male Scaup (**9**) shows a pale back and broad white wing bar and look a little heavier in flight than the Tufted Duck. The female (**10**) is very like the female Tufted Duck unless the greater amount of white on the face can be seen.

The male of the Tufted Duck (**11**) is more lightly built than the male Scaup and has less white on the wing than the Ferruginous Duck. The female (**12**) is very similar to the Scaup but not as white underneath as the female Ferruginous Duck.

The male Harlequin's patterning of white and blue-grey (**13**) are conspicuous in flight, plus a short white wing bar bordering a purple speculum. The female (**14**) has no wing bar and a pale belly not white as in the Long-tailed Duck.

The large white patches on the inner wing of the male Bufflehead (**15**), and its black and white head on a white neck, are entirely distinctive. The female (**16**) has white secondaries and a conspicuous white patch on the side of the head.

The male Barrow's Goldeneye (**17**) needs careful separation from the Goldeneye. It has less extensive white on the wings with a dividing black line, as well as more white on the face. The female (**18**) has a darker forewing than the Goldeneye but is otherwise almost identical.

The extensive white on the wing of the male Goldeneye (**19**) resembles the Bufflehead, which, however, has white on the back of the head. Separation from Barrow's Goldeneye is also possible using this feature. The female (**20**) has two panels of white on the secondaries and a pale grey forewing.

White-headed Ducks have fast wing-beats. The male (**21**) lacks any wing bar and identification from Ruddy Duck must be based on the large head and swollen bill. The female (**22**) also is without a wing bar, and has grey-brown underparts.

The Ruddy Duck also has a rather whirring wing action. Males (**23**) have no wing bars and can only be separated from White-headed Ducks on the shape and pattern of the head. The female (**24**) has pale or whitish underparts.

2. Adult breeding plumage

Eiders are broad and short-winged in flight silhouette. The male (**1**) is black and white and with a smaller head than the other species of eiders. The female (**2**) is brown overall with a very faint wing bar in front of the obscure speculum.

The male King Eider (**3**) has a large white panel on the forewing and a dark leading edge. The female (**4**) has a slightly more pronounced whitish wing bar than the female Eider.

The Spectacled Eider male (**5**) in flight has a narrow dark leading edge and a white back, more like an Eider than the King Eider, apart from the different head shape. The female (**6**) has virtually no wing bar and a pale mark round the eye.

The white forewing and sides of the back of the male Steller's Eider (**7**) and its mainly white head and dark chest-band make it quite unlike any other duck. The female (**8**) shows a double white wing bar and the underwing is strikingly white.

Only the white on the head distinguishes the male Surf Scoter (**9**) from the male Common Scoter. The head pattern also has to be seen on the female (**10**) to separate it from the same species.

The male Long-tailed Duck (**11** — in winter plumage) is completely distinctive with its white head and neck and very long tail. The female (**12**) has a lot of white on the face and white underparts, which distinguish it from female Harlequins.

Common Scoter males (**13**) are black all over showing no white on head or wing. The females (**14**) have white cheeks and chin to separate them from female Surf Scoters.

The Velvet Scoter male (**15**) is black with a brilliant white panel on the secondaries, which immediately separates it from the other scoters. The female (**16**) similarly has white on the secondaries unlike any other brown duck.

The black and white barring on the wing and back of the male Smew (**17**) gives it a pied appearance, while the white head and neck are equally distinctive. The female (**18**) also has a lot of white on the wing, but rather obscured by two brown bars.

The crest of the Hooded Merganser (**19**) goes flat in flight but the black and white pattern is still obvious and the head looks large. The wing is barred black and white. The female (**20**) has a noticeably barred white speculum.

Male Goosanders (**21**) show pure white inner wings and dark outer halves. Apart from the dark head, back and wing tips, the rest is white. The female (**22**) has a broad white speculum crossed by an incomplete dark bar and a pale grey forewing.

The male Red-breasted Merganser (**23**) has the white on the wings broken by dark bars, and a dark chest bar. Both help to separate it from male Goosanders. The female (**24**) also has a dark bar dividing the white on its wings, and a darker forewing than the Goosander female.

N.W.CUSA.

Index

Page numbers for descriptions accompanied by plates are in bold type, thus: **24**.

Boundary of the Western Palearctic

Land over 450 metres (1500 feet)

0   200   400   600   800   1000 miles

0   400   800   1200   1600 km

N O R T H   A T L A N T I C

Newfoundland

Azores

Madeira

Canary Is.

C. Blanc

Banc d'Arguin

Cape Verde Is.

MAURITANIA

SÉNÉGAL

M A L I

PORTUGAL

SPAIN

Douro

Ebr

Tagus

Guadiana

MOROCCO

A L G E R

IR